AF587532

RADICAL

A publication by *forty five degrees*
Edited by Elise Misao Hunchuck

PUNCH

RITUALS

CONTENTS

My contention is that lives are led not inside places but through, around, to and, from there, from and to places elsewhere. I use the term wayfaring to describe the embodied experience of this perambulatory movement. [...] Proceeding along a path, every inhabitant lays a trail. Where inhabitants meet, trails are entwined, as the life of each becomes bound up with the other.

– Tim Ingold

Against Space: Place, Movement, Knowledge

Radical Rituals is an itinerant survey along the 45°N parallel between 45°N 1°W and 45°N 35°E. It is a study of the inventiveness of everyday life, new spatial practices, and vernacular rituals that stimulate and nurture *commons* across Europe.

This project focuses on beings, situated scenarios, and collaborative actions in order to review current vocabularies and methods of spatial production. In the present socio-political situation, there is an urge to re-imagine methods of spatial practices and pay attention to more complex understandings of the interwoven relations between humans, nonhumans, and the effects of physical contexts. To do this, we follow an imaginary line: the 45°N parallel. This line crosses Europe, from the Atlantic Coast to the Black Sea. Through field trips and interactions with local actors, we disrupt the line's abstraction and challenge symbolic perceptions of reductive dichotomies such as the center/periphery, north/south, and east/west. This topographic approach allows us to study the 45°N parallel through rituals, collective organizational structures, and non-commercial activities that address global topics like climate justice, gender, biodiversity, degrowth, and solidarity, providing the best possible responses to their local contexts. More just spatial practices are to be found in the diversity and nuances of myriad space-making paradigms. These practices are named *rituals* because they strengthen the potential for collective action to reach systemic changes. They are labeled *radical* because they are highly transformative and point to possible futures. Good examples can inform our practice as architects, urban planners, landscape architects and researchers.

From the shared experiences, research, and workshops emerged this publication series: Radical Rituals 45°N 1°W – 45°N 35°E. These pages feature the mapping of landscapes and initiatives, while a series of collaborative essays enrich and contextualize the topics discussed. Radical Rituals 45°N 1°W – 45°N 35°E gathers local projects along this line to contribute to a dynamic network comprised of the multiple existing conditions that are encouraging and maintaining alternative spatial configurations in Europe. At the end of this journey, the experiences and data collected–the region, the landscape, the local practices–will be connected to national and international contexts to reflect upon the future of spatial practice.

TOWARDS A NEW SPACE-MAKING PARADIGM

Through Radical Rituals, we want to contribute to the discussion on how to generate and foster alternative spatial paradigms and new modes of thinking and making as critical alternatives to the alienation, exploitation, and commodification of common space. The overwhelming complexity of our times has weakened our capacity to think otherwise, leaving us with–and within–a design crisis. The spatial practices, in their different forms–design, architecture, and city planning–need a profound revision of their methods, resources, and means. As Marina Otero Verzier suggests:

"In this context, current generations have the duty to design possible futures and forms of existence that are not based on extractive technologies and economies and conceive spaces for collective organisation and find common grounds for action."[1] Through case studies and field trips, we travel and document stories of diverse local space-making initiatives and the complex networks they are part of. They are tales and recollections that move beyond disciplinary boundaries, and they challenge comfortable, hegemonic narratives of space production.

A new space-making paradigm can grow in the fertile gap between *emergency* and *emergence*. This investigation looks to the rituals arising from actions and conditions across territories, focusing on spatial frameworks for conviviality. The methodology for this exploration is based on spatial analysis deployed across multiple scales: beings, actions,

1 Marina Otero Verzier, "Turning the Tables: Architecture after architecture," in *Archifutures Vol. 6: Agency*, eds. Sophie Lovell and George Kafka, & beyond collective (Barcelona: dpr-barcelona, 2020), 41.

contexts and physical spaces. Through travel, this research expands networks and knowledge, enhances vocabularies and collaborations around Europe and it reassesses our practice by adapting existing local techniques and solutions to develop non-disciplinary methods.

The diverse formats in which the project unfolds allow the public to engage with the content in various approaches, making it accessible regardless of background or expertise. The aim is to enable a thread of collective thinking, where any one interested in related topics can contribute and interact with the overall research process. These interactions will spark connections and provoke new thoughts from the local to a continental scale. How do we learn from existing spatial methods to transmit their qualities of distributed knowledge, enhance its potential for systemic change?

By bringing the term *radical* into relation with *rituals*, we want to question what 'radical design' is today—and in the future.[2] Radical design must engage with more than resources, spaces, or places. It must entangle more diverse agents—human and non-human—and their interactions, drawing attention to the networks that shape our world. Who are the space-makers that nurture the commons and blur the boundaries of professional and academic practices? This research studies and brings together the makers and the conditions that nurture the *radical rituals*, both individual and collective, that are imagining more just spatial practices.

2 In 1972 Emilio Ambasz curated *Italy: The New Domestic Landscape. Achievements and Problems of Italian Design* at the Museum of Modern Art (MoMA) in New York. An assemblage of avant-garde designers from Italy including UFO, Superstudio, Ugo La Pietra, and Ettore Sottsass, among many others, converged to generate a radical narrative of design, revising its methods, tools, and means under the rubric of 'Radical Design.' This watershed reference is the starting point for our critical review of architecture and design.

RADICAL RITUALS
45°N 20°E – 45°N 31°E

As architects and urban planners, we have learned and developed our work in a society in which a simplistic understanding of space as either public or private prevails. Accordingly, spatial practice is almost always executed under commodified conditions. Current spatial designs are driven by efficiency and profit, where space is often exploited. Nonetheless, life cannot be restricted to binary notions. Inevitably, ways of living transcend the boundaries of classifications and emerge in all of their entangled complexity. In Radical Rituals, we explore the role of design in imagining and producing spaces that contain other, more nuanced and exploratory forms of living. It is from this standpoint that we focus on practices of commoning–*commons*–that enable more sustainable and equitable uses ofresources than the market and state can provide.[1]

Decades of neoliberal policies prioritizing profit over people, the evident obsolescence of public services, mismanagement of migratory

1 Please see Massimo De Angelis' *Omnia Sunt Communia: On the Commons and the Transformation to Postcapitalism* (London: Bloomsbury Publishing, 2017).

movements, and, perhaps most urgent, the failure to address climate change in a coordinated manner demonstrate the need to revolutionize the way we manage and envision our common spaces. At a time when the "system that converts relationships to services and commons to commodities"[2], we want to investigate the potential of collective non-disciplinary practices to meet contemporary ecological, economic, and societal challenges. Our research project, Radical Rituals, attempts to imagine how spatial practice can reinvent itself to uphold such a complex venture. This book-as-itinerant-survey speculates on the contemporary role of borders, economies, and identities in the framework of the European continent.

Europe is a hybrid place in constant mutation, shaped by movements of people, knowledge, and goods, with multiple climates, geographies, languages, and policies marked by socio-economic and geopolitical struggles.

2 Phineas Harper, "Our dependency on growth, like on concrete, must be abolished," *Dezeen*, September 25, 2019, https://www.dezeen.com/2019/09/25/oslo-architecture-triennale-architecture-degrowth-phineas-harper

The so-called 'European Integration' strategies from the Coal and Steel Community (1951) and the European Economic Community (1957) to the culmination of the European Union (EU) in the Treaty of Maastricht (1992) were developed over the span of many years, focusing mainly on the promotion of free markets.[3] In the process, Eastern and Southern countries have been left aside, with existing stereotypes reinforced in relation to specific and symbolic understandings of space, including center/periphery, north/south, and east/west. In the meantime, the EU has doubled in size, launched an international currency, and steadily boosted its GDP. In contrast, it has weakened national powers without consolidating supra-national sovereignty and left political leaders adrift in an often-ill-defined limbo between the two. Consequently, European culture and values have been developed under the abstract idea of a so-called 'European condition.' If the consolidation of a young European society identifies

3 As Andrew Moravcsik bluntly affirms in his book, *The Choice for Europe: Social Purpose and State Power from Messina to Maastricht* (Ithaca, NY: Cornell University Press, 1998, 11): "the EU is basically about business."

a gap between local necessities across the so-called 'old continent' and the European project (a gap that includes the polarization between north and south, east and west, heterogeneous economic models, and a diversity of cultural and historical backgrounds), then projects such as The New European Bauhaus or The New Green Deal highlight their own disconnection from territorial specificities and local identities.[4]

Radical Rituals is determined to find the connective tissue between abstract ideas and situated vernacular conditions and practices across regions and peoples.[5] Bordeaux, Briançon, Turin, Belgrade, Pula, Bucharest, Tulcea, and Simferopol are the starting points of our research, and the list of proposed locations is continuously evolving. Radical Rituals unveil the micro-politics of the land[6]: this exercise

4 In recent years, critical debates around hegemonic European narratives have taken place, including in the academic context, such as at the Jan Van Eyck Akademie: https://www.janvaneyck.nl/projects/debating-the-new-european-bauhaus

5 Donna Haraway. "Situated Knowledges: The Science Question in Feminism and the Privilege of Partial Perspective," *Feminist Studies*, Vol. 14, no. 3 (Autumn, 1988): 575-599.

6 Michel Foucault. "Of Other Spaces: Utopias and Heterotopias," *Architecture/Mouvement/Continuité* (October, 1984). Originally published under the title *Des Espace Autres* and translated from French by Jay Miskowiec.

calls forward the relevance of our atmospheric knowledge[7] and how it shapes our ways of living as we ask the following questions: what are the specific spatial conditions of each case study? Which relations are created within a space, landscape, or region concerning a specific community? And how might we articulate these variable conditions in a comprehensive and critical archive of cases that can be activated to enhance current discourses? Our interest extends beyond political borders, where the friction of diversity and its generative power can invent new modes of coexistence.

In *The Garden in Motion*, Gilles Clément introduces *wild spatial voids* as potential spaces for reinventing design practice.[8] Clément considers the generally neglected spaces of the city where spontaneous, natural processes and wildness can evolve. On these sites, non-human, non-utilitarian processes allow for diversity, uncertainty, and serendipity. It is a fertile territory for species to arise, emerge

7 Gernot Böhme. *Atmospheric Architectures: The Aesthetics of Felt Spaces* (London: Bloomsbury Publishing, 2017).
8 Gilles Clement. *El Jardín en Movimiento* (Barcelona: Gustavo Gili, 2012).

and consolidate. Clément introduces the *third landscape* as a design-based response to engage with these vivid places of flourishment. The garden in motion, and the living plots, each allow the designer to be immersed in the midst of this natural transformation. Through attentive execution, the design enriches the space in a sympoietic relationship with nature, rather than aggressively intervening with it, erasing previous traces.[9] This constant dialogue and response-ability of the design process described by Clément is crucial for caring for the things and beings that emerge from the spontaneous ecology.[10] This wildness resists the idea of an enclosed space executed under top-down strategies. It has helped

9 Beth Dempster. "Sympoietic and autopoietic systems: A new distinction for self-organising systems." Waterloo: School of Planning, University of Waterloo. https://www.semanticscholar.org/paper/SYMPOIETIC-AND-AUTOPOIETIC-SYSTEMS%3A-A-NEW-FOR-Dempster/44299317a20afcd33b0a11d3b2bf4fc196088d45

10 According to Donna Haraway in her book, *Staying with the Trouble: Making Kin in the Chthulucene*, the network might emerge in manifold ways by cultivating 'response-ability': "Response-ability is about both absence and presence, killing and nurturing, living and dying–and remembering of who lives and who dies and how in the string figures of natural cultural history." For more, please see Haraway's *Staying with the Trouble: Making Kin in the Chthulucene* (Durham/London: Duke University Press, 2016).

us conceive of our interactions as designers of such a garden, encouraging us to ask how to apply this design method elsewhere.

The diversity of our world flourishes precisely in these *threshold spaces*[11]: every situated scenario brings nuances and novel conditions to the ways all relations, human, non-human, and spatial, are established through collective negotiations, rituals, and social choreographies.[12] Collective behaviors are the primal matter shaping patterns in spatial thresholds: an experience of habitation that challenges and blurs the modernist definitions of function-form, giving birth to new frameworks and possibilities. Spatial practices that allow for this wildness and approach urban space as a process follow Stavrides' notion of "urban porosity." Beyond private and public, "Porosity articulates urban life, while it also loosens the borders erected to preserve a strict

11 Please see the chapter "Space and potentialities of space commoning. The capacity to act and think through space" in Stavros Stavrides' *Common Spaces of Urban Emancipation* (Manchester: Manchester University Press, 2019).

12 Isabelle Stengers, "An Ecology of Practices" (lecture, ANU Humanities Research Centre Symposium, August, 2003).

spatial and temporal social order."[13] Practices of *commoning* are fundamental to our study as a generative method.

Visualizing and producing a network of *threshold spaces* can collectively shape a sort of *urban porosity*. However, imagining porosity in architecture leaves us with important questions: who performs those practices that configure common spaces, and under what conditions? With this research, we present an assemblage of examples within the European context, in which numerous actors are working, through a multiplicity of boundaries, to define *commons* in situated manners. Across spatial scales, these actors enable contexts of negotiation and response-ability, as opposed to rigid paradigms, shaping physically and politically their worlds. This study gathers examples with two main objectives: to redefine the methods and qualities of spatial practice

13 Please see Stavros Stavrides, "Heterotopias and the Experience of Porous Urban Space," in *Loose Space: Possibility and Diversity in Urban Life*, eds. Karen A. Franck and Quentin Stevens (London: Routledge, 2007) 174–192.

and create a network of rituals. Silvia Federici describes these subtle affinities and gestures where everyday life brings us together on the very act of making and living as "commoning with a small c."[14]

Rituals lead to the crystallization of such collective patterns, behaviors, and ways of thinking at a socio-political level. They traverse the different scales of society (individual, private, and public) and create ties of kinship and identity until they become *habitus*.[15] Therefore, we focus on the inventiveness of everyday life, and, borrowing from Georges Perec, we look for infra-ordinary experiences, extensions of the relation between beings, behaviors, spaces, and policies.[16] *Rituals* provide a non-disciplinary model for design, expanding the limits and notions of spatial practice by engaging all agents, regardless

14 Silvia Federici. "Feminism and the politics of the commons." *The Commoner* (June 2020). https://thecommoner.org/wp-content/uploads/2020/06/federici-feminism-and-the-politics-of-commons.pdf

15 Marcel Mauss defined *habitus* as those aspects of culture that are anchored in the body or daily practices of individuals, groups, societies, or nations.

16 Georges Perec. *Species of Spaces and Other Pieces* (London: Penguin Classics, 2008).

of their discipline and level of expertise.[17] If we understand spatial production as collective action, these patterns open up a liminal space where emergent habits—not yet consolidated—allow for imagining transformative spatial paradigms. Through this investigation, we propose new terminologies in response to our findings, with the aim of expanding the current vocabulary of architecture and design and recognizing the innovative value of distributed knowledge. What is the potential of rituals for triggering a common awareness of spatial agency?[18] What kinds of spatial typologies and organizational models might arise?

Radical Rituals 45°N 20°E – 45°N 31°E is the first iteration of this ongoing research. For three weeks, and in the context of Romania, we visited and studied several examples of radical practices that transform spatial configurations and contribute to the local public discourse. Over twenty initiatives and agents were documented. Traveling physically to

17 Joi Ito and Jeff Howe. *Whiplash: How to Survive Our Faster Future* (Massachusetts: MIT Press, 2016).
18 Nishat Awan, Tatjana Schneider, and Jeremy Till. *Spatial Agency: Other Ways of Doing Architecture* (London: Routledge, 2011).

the location of each initiative is crucial to the project. As a method, it enables us to identify the micro-politics of each context while creating affective bonds with the people we meet. Through conversations about necessities, methods, and forms of direct action, knowledge around design practice is informed directly from local sources. These radical rituals present alternative spatial paradigms based on assemblages of beings, practices, experiences, and social performativity across spatial and social scales.[19] The question we pose from iteration to iteration is, how can spatial production be an emancipatory project for societies?

We are interested in the publication format as a tangible medium for collecting, sharing knowledge, and reflecting upon different perspectives and voices associated with the local context of each stretch of the line. These first written reflections should be conceived as a travelogue. Here, we gathered stories, encounters, landscapes, and findings

19 Bojana Cvejic and Ana Vujanovic. *Public Sphere by Performance* (Berlin: b_books, 2012).

of our field trip. The travelogue emphasizes the concerns and valuable work of all the agents involved, as well as the experiences and atmospheric conditions of our journey. The topics we encounter are multifaceted and complex, and by no means do we intend to draw conclusions. Rather, we want to open up our suitcases and share thoughts and novel narratives to trigger further discussions. The stories, conversations, and featured projects are significant to us in their specificity and intricate connections with worldwide topics. All knowledge assembled participates in a network of thinking where solutions and possibilities are all respected and cared for similarly—regardless of the background or status of the project.

This publication is structured into three main chapters based on narrative threads that reoccurred throughout our encounters. The objective of this research is not to preconceive general topics and apply them to situated scenarios but, instead, to broaden the framework of study by encouraging and then analyzing narratives that emerge from local agents telling us the stories of their initiatives.[20] The underlying initiatives brought these topics to our table, and we have worked to incorporate them transversally. The categorization comes out of a sensitive process of listening to, conversing with, and observing specific qualities: spatial, organizational, relational, and political.[21] This process allowed us to find three narratives: *commons*, *waters,* and *identities*. In each chapter, the topics take the form of interviews, articles, and featured initiatives.

The first chapter is dedicated to *commons,* a topic central to our explorations due to its potency in generating non-hegemonic structures and narratives and opening spaces for negotiation. Most of the projects gathered in

20 When we use the term 'local agents,' we are referring to the protagonists of our stories; the people we get in touch with from each project. These groups actively engage with individuals and communities through action-based responses. Their broad knowledge of specific problems, methods, and solutions has also become our primary source of knowledge. We recognize and welcome the subjectivity they bring to possible outcomes; this is also why we understand ourselves as collecting stories and perspectives and not merely conclusions or academic statements.

21 Here, we are thinking about 'attentive tending' by way of the methodology outlined by Soft Agency. For more, please see Teresa Dillon's "Methodologies of Softness," Copenhagen *Architecture Festival Journal*, August 24, 2021, https://www.cafx.dk/post/methodologies-of-softness

this publication are developing, to a certain extent, forms of *commoning*, and they illustrate the nuances and possibilities of this broad concept. Although it is an issue of increasing global interest, it is essential to understand the meaning of *commons* in a highly situated manner, particularly in the context of Romania and its communist past. It is for this reason, that we invited Alex Axinte to open this book with his investigation of *urban commons*, as we found it vital to understand its meaning in the Romanian context. In place of developing a universal model, his approach toward commons is grounded in local Romanian stories and socio-economic and political practices. In Romania, specific historical post-communist narratives influence how the community relates to public and private spaces: there is a general mistrust of public administrations and, in most cases, a withdrawal of their management of public assets leading to an extreme liberalization of land in the last thirty years. These rooted factors make it extremely difficult for actions of *commoning* to start,

let alone to succeed. Through his text, Alex frames the conditions that enable collective practices in the urban context, despite past and present hindrances.

In a *conversation* with Alexandra Trofin, head of BETA, the Timișoara Architecture Biennial, we discuss the city as a common good and the role of the biennial as a platform for empowering visions of a more sustainable shared future. In an *article* about Stația Experimentală de Cercetare pentru Artă și Viață (The Experimental Research Station for Art and Life), we reflect on the idea of expanded communities, their networks and resilience, and the means of cultural production in the current crisis. The three *featured projects,* Grupul de Inițiativă Civică Cișmigiu (Cișmigiu Civic Initiative Group), Asociația Culturală și Ecologică SEPALE (SEPALE Cultural and Ecological Association), and Atelier Ad Hoc Arhitectura expand the framework and vocabularies of commonality, and they provide us with examples of how to reconnect communities in spatial thresholds.

Their works strive to rebuild notions of belonging with and awareness of the environment that can evolve into responsibility and care for common spaces and multispecies coexistence.

The topic of *waters* unfolds in a transscalar way, connecting local geographic scenarios with the continental landscape. The Danube is the main riverine water body of Europe; it flows through Central and Southeastern Europe, beginning in the Black Forest of Germany and ending where it meets the Black Sea. The Danube River and its delta move through Romania from the northwest border with Hungary and Serbia, tracing the border with Bulgaria to the south. The biotopes that make up the river and its delta traverse issues and disciplines such as geography, sociology, and biology, and they carry with them concerns around waste management and water pollution, maintenance of biodiversity, and water bodies as a common civic good. All of these are interwoven topics, and they recur in the works of local initiatives that span the river's territory.

The river and other 'common goods' in Romania fall into the spaces that emerge between private and public spheres: Who owns the river? Who cares for it?

After the fall of the communist regime, the extreme liberalization and over thirty years of privatization that followed resulted in a lack of regulation in public services and the maintenance of waterscapes, giving form to anomalous relationships between the water bodies and their residents. Across Romania the river banks are widely privatized and are, in many places, hard to access. The river has disappeared from the imagination of residents as a natural landscape or a public space that could be accessible to all. It is becoming a place to be used, as a dump or a site of resource extraction. Along the regions and climates it crosses, civic groups address issues of local urgency that are also of global relevance; their actions raise possible solutions, and they influence governmental action on Romanian river policies.

In a *conversation* with Loredana Pană, we discuss the socio-economic and ecological vulnerability of the Danube Delta. Someș Delivery's *article* revindicates the right to use river banks as public areas for leisure and life while engaging with students and local agents, creating a platform for shared knowledge. The work of *featured projects* like Asociația 37, MaiMultVerde (More Green), and Răzvan Crimschi ranges from educational programs to policy-making negotiations to protect the Danube's ecosystem and restore free access to clean waters.

The third chapter focuses on *identities*, one of the most decisive and challenging issues of our conflicted time. Identities are the intangible commons of societies; they shape collective behaviors and thoughts and are fundamental in the emergence of rituals. Spatially, identities can be reflected in local architectural typologies, where possibly the most quintessential representation is architectural heritage. Identity constantly changes and moves through temporalities and cultures; it is strongly connected to affections and memories, yet difficult to be transformed or redefined. Today, efficiency and globalization homogenize spatial and social identities. Local identities are, thus, temporal and continuously subject to change. Preservation and maintenance by residents are crucial for them to last. The vulnerability of such practices is notable, particularly where a scarcity of resources makes it difficult for them to endure. And while it is true that projects frequently disappear due to a lack of funding or the exhaustion of those involved actors, it is also true that because time and the consolidation of identities in transformation are intimately related, sustaining them is possible when they are rooted in societal patterns.

In a *conversation* with Mihai Danciu, we get a comprehensive overview of the identity and current issues in the development of the Banat region, a place that transverses the borders of Romania, Serbia, and Hungary, and whose economic and socio-cultural development showcase the substratal connections

of shared values and forms of living exceeding current political borders. An *article* on Ambulanța Pentru Monumente (Ambulance for Monuments), also in Banat, focuses on built heritage and how, through an educational approach, non-governmental organizations are taking care of and maintaining regional heritage. *Featured projects* such as those of Casa Verde (Green House), Aici Acolo Pop-Up Gallery, and h.arta address the impact of historical backgrounds and heritage on contemporary ways of living; thus, the importance of local crafts and new cultural production in the face of current challenges concerning local and global, urban and rural, or present and past identities affect specific contexts.

This publication is the beginning of an extensive conversation, a place for exchange, and a first attempt to come together, to think together, and to share these voices and stories with a wider audience. Radical Rituals 45°N 20°E – 45°N 31°E is the first round of travels and the beginning of a compendium of publications along the 45°N parallel. In the iterations to follow, other places and stories will be added as we follow the line and widen our conversations through France, Italy, Croatia, Serbia, and Bosnia-Herzegovina. Our research methodology will continue to embrace non-disciplinary approaches to knowledge production. The Radical Rituals publication series is not an academic, theoretical body of work. Instead, we choose to engage in varied investigations that encompass multiple narratives, making and keeping space for inclusion and diversity. This enables us to share the many voices already actively contributing to current architectural and spatial discourses.

The project's goal is to envision a future of spatial practice that is more just: our aim is to be inclusive, plural, ambitious, and visionary. We investigate the soft systems of cities and landscapes, the potential of local communities, heritage, imaginaries, and practices that encourage new forms of collectivity. We seek to unfold the complexities of our world and assess novel conditions of spatial agency. The following texts share our physical journey and present the means and methods of the featured projects found along the way. From 45°N 20°E to 45°N 31°E, we assembled a compendium of transformative examples to create places for reflection, spaces for wonder, and alliances for alternative futures. We hope you enjoy reading them as much as we enjoyed learning with and writing about them.

Wholeheartedly,
forty five degrees

RITUALS OF LIVING TOGETHER: URBAN COMMONS IN BUCLĂ (THE LOOP)

● 44° 26’N – 26° 05’E

by Alex Axinte

Previous page. Top image: Come Out to the Trailer! A two-day event during which activities from the Garage space were taken out onto the main boulevard, Buclă (the Loop), as part of the street festival, Street Delivery 2021. Hosted by the Trailer of Research and Activation (RCA). Drumul Taberei, 2021.

Bottom image: The care for green spaces gained momentum in the 1970s and 1980s, when, encouraged by the state, inhabitants set up productive gardens around their buildings and on individually allotted plots. Drumul Taberei, 1984.

After the fall of the Berlin wall, the thirty years of neoliberal policies that followed transformed post-socialist societies and their urban settings. Despite this, collective housing neighborhoods, built during the socialist period, still dominate housing options, as they continue to host most of Romania's urban population. These neighborhoods are facing radical privatization, collapsing public infrastructure, and rampant individualization. Their civic spaces, including parks, public libraries, or cultural facilities, are fragmented and underfinanced. Here, public spaces are constantly eroded, enclosed, and commodified, fueled by a dominant narrative praising entrepreneurship and private initiative. At the same time, excessive financialization has transformed housing from a basic right into a meritocracy based on economic privilege.[1] This evolution has left post-socialist cities unprepared for today's social, environmental and economic challenges. However, elements of the public

1 Liviu Chelcea and Oana Druţă, "Zombie Socialism and the Rise of Neoliberalism in Post-Socialist Central and Eastern Europe," *Eurasian Geography and Economics* 57, no. 4–5 (September 2, 2016): 521–44.

grid from the initial projects of radical urbanization are still in place. The need for care and repair appeals to basic or "latent" commoning processes[2] among city dwellers. Moreover, specific practices of living together, based on solidarity and spatial appropriation and forged in times of crisis and restraint have developed and even thrived. These specific elements of the post-socialist city have the capacity to act as key elements for localized solutions in regeneration processes.

In this context, the latitudinal dérive of *forty five degrees* Radical Rituals project elicits situated questions rather than merely pinning down prefabricated answers. Their curiosity traces some of the current themes at stake in diverse local contexts by looking over the European project's East-West or North-South conceptual divides. One of the results of the meetings between their gaze and local practices was the need for narratives beyond dominant ones. More than just a desire for storytelling, these action-based (self-)narratives have

2 Massimo De Angelis, *Omnia Sunt Communia: On the Commons and the Transformation to Postcapitalism* (London: Zed Books, 2017).

the potential of deconstruction for the reconstruction of a shared vision of the world. In this case, the narratives attempt to illustrate what brings together the diverse material and immaterial ingredients of the post-socialist city. What makes living together possible, despite grim projections? What do we give to, and what do we take from our streets and neighborhoods? How can we contribute, and what can we share as communities of dwellers?

This text expands on the fieldwork experiences of my practice-based Ph.D. The research aims to evidence the concept of urban commons from the perspective of an engaged practice set in the context of collective housing estates. Commoning practices are evidenced through the case study research and activation project Garaj DESCHIS (OPEN Garage) project,[3] set in the Drumul Taberei neighborhood of Bucharest, Romania.

3 OPEN Garage was initiated in 2020 by Alex Axinte as part of his Ph.D. fieldwork. In 2021, after receiving a grant from the Romanian Order of Architects, the research activities and team were expanded to include: Bogdan Iancu (anthropologist), Iris Șerban (anthropologist), Anca Niță (sociologist), Ileana Szasz (director), Diana Culescu (landscape designer), Ioana Tudora (architect), Ioana Irinciuc (librarian).

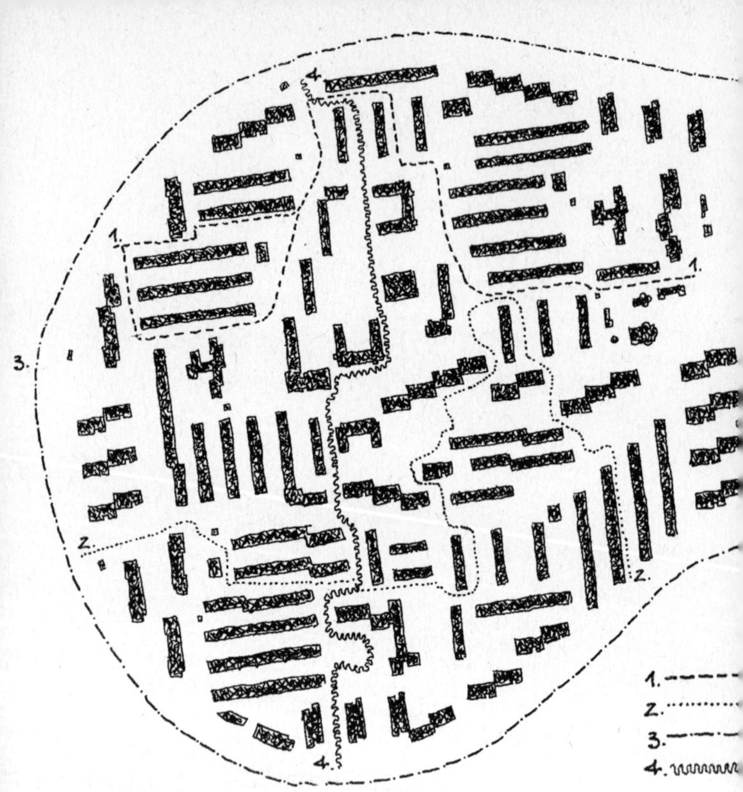

This map of Buclă (the Loop) proposes four exploratory routes: 1. The inner street includes services and corner shops; 2. The informal green spaces of the block's gardens; 3. Alternative graphics of block street art; 4. Through the school yard, a space for play and sport.

URBAN COMMONS IN THE POST-SOCIALIST CITY: NESTED IN THE GRID

In recent years, the commons narrative has gained momentum. Going beyond state and market,[4] most definitions of commons account for three interdependent components: the resources, the community, and the governance.[5] Applied to the city, the more traditional rural extraction model of the commons falls short, calling for a 'new' commons paradigm adapted to the institutional ecosystem of the city.[6] Urban commons become an alternative socio-political proposition, enabling a more democratic, just, and sustainable society. Processes of commoning, enacted through various local collective living patterns, articulate implicit and explicit ways of resistance to the hegemonic paradigm of individualization and marketization.

4 Elinor Ostrom, *Governing the Commons: The Evolution of Institutions for Collective Action*, Canto Classics (Cambridge: Cambridge University Press, 2015).

5 Urban Commons Research Collective, *The Urban Commons Handbook*. (Barcelona: dpr Barcelona, 2022).

6 Stavros Stavrides, *Common Spaces of Urban Emancipation* (Manchester: Manchester University Press, 2019).

Urban commons are not just an exportable model, or a package of formal organization structure, with administrative and legislative measures which can be universally applied. Commons are also a way of life situated in diverse local contexts. In the post-socialist city, the urban commons can be identified as supported by an inherited but fragmented public grid, thus evidencing Elinor Ostrom's 'nestedness' principle. Iaione and Foster consider this principle a condition for the commons' manifestation within the complex institutional system of the city.[7] This broken and threatened public grid needs repair, maintenance, and support, triggering collaboration, care, and repair among its users. This need activates what De Angelis calls "latent" commons already existing in society. As an alternative living pattern to pursuing profit, these latent forms of commoning, such as "loyalty to friends, conviviality, mutual aid and even struggles"[8], can be further developed

7 Christian Iaione and Sheila R Foster, "Ostrom in the City: Design Principles for the Urban Commons," 2017, https://www.thenatureofcities.com/2017/08/20/ostrom-city-design-principles-urban-commons.

8 Ibid, 2.

into systemic patterns of explicit commoning. With the governance formula being less explicit, latent commoning can be detected in the post-socialist city, derived from patterns of living together. Commoning elements are performed in everyday acts and they can become modern rituals forged in specific historical and spatial local contexts. Adopting and perpetuating such rituals allows city dwellers to recognize each other, develop a sense of belonging to the community, and manifest their attachment to their neighborhoods. This phenomenon is perhaps more evident in the context of large collective housing neighborhoods, the dominant form of urban housing in the post-socialist city.

COLLECTIVE HOUSING NEIGHBORHOODS

A few decades of abrupt industrialization radically transformed the previously socialist Romania from overwhelmingly rural to mostly urban.[9] The population of Bucharest, the

9 With 76% rural population in 1948, Romania reaches 54% urban population in 1992. Found in INS, "Baze de Date Statistice," 2018, http://statistici.insse.ro:8077/tempo-online/#/pages/tables/insse-table.

Drumul Taberei Monograph. Neighborhood streets were used as spaces to explore, play, participate and create. Drumul Taberei, 1973.

capital city of Romania, increased rapidly.[10] Starting in the 1960s, a massive "urban systematisation" process transformed the city by developing large collective housing estates. The socialist state's subsidized housing–or collective housing–was "an integral part of the labor economy"[11], accommodating the workforce for the urban factories and the emerging middle class of the state's service sector. Housing and its communal infrastructure became an incentive for attracting the new dwellers to move into the cities. These neighborhoods, intended as housing for all, were qualitatively different from the social housing of their Western counterparts: apartments were allocated off the market and were the only available form of modern urban housing during socialism.

After 1989, anti-communism became the main ideological discourse of the "transition period," understood "not as a temporary state (...) but a form and a freestanding political

10 The population of Bucharest grew by 100% between 1948 and 1992, moving above 2 million inhabitants. Found in Ibid, 9.

11 Ivan Szelenyi, "Urban Development and Regional Management in Eastern Europe," Theory and Society 10, no. 2 (March 1981): 169–205, https://doi.org/10.1007/BF00139891.

problem".[12] This new hegemonic narrative allowed neoliberal politics to thrive, leading to massive changes in the post-socialist city, such as the radical privatization of the collective housing apartments.[13] Welcomed by the frustrated tenants of the former socialist state, the owner status was the most precious "gift of the revolution."[14] Despite the state's retreat, massive privatization, and chronic underfinancing, these neighborhoods proved resilient, recently "enjoying something of a renaissance."[15] The roots of this phenomenon can be traced to the previously contested

12 Florin Poenaru, *Locuri comune: clasă, anticomunism, stânga* (Tact, 2017). Translated by Alex Axinte.

13 Bucharest reached a "super-home-ownership" of 98%, Romania having the highest rate of home-ownership in the EU. See more in Alice Pittini et al., "The State of Housing in EU in 2017" (Housing Europe, the European Federation of Public, Cooperative and Social Housing, October 2017), http://www.housingeurope.eu/resource-1000/the-state-of-housing-in-the-eu-2017.

14 Vintilă Mihăilescu, "Public Şi Privat În Bucureşti. O Introducere.," in *Societatea Reală, Volumul 2, Of, Bucureştii Mei*, ed. Vintila Mihailescu (Bucuresti: Paidea, 2005).

15 The privatization of public utilities networks, coupled with the badly needed modernization of the buildings and the management of communal infrastructure, is left mostly to the tenant's associations, which lack the tools, skills, and resources to cope with these systemic shifts, managing just to keep the buildings afloat. Vera Marin and Liviu Chelcea, "The Many (Still) Functional Housing Estates of Bucharest, Romania: A Viable Housing Provider in Europe's Densest Capital City," in *Housing Estates in Europe*, ed. Daniel Baldwin Hess, Tiit Tammaru, and Maarten van Ham, The Urban Book Series (Cham: Springer International Publishing, 2018), 167–90.

socialist project of "social engineering," which allowed these neighborhoods to achieve today a social mixing in support of a healthy urbanity.[16] Also, the 2008 financial crisis showed the limits of the highly individualistic housing proposition, contributing to reconsidering the collective estates built in socialism.

Furthermore, a rise in public investment in building insulation, new playgrounds, and maintained green areas, marked their return to the public agenda. Moreover, their inherited relational networks, practiced since the initial workers-neighbors developed a specific pattern of living, contributed to their rejuvenation. Coping with systemic changes, demographic transformations, and exacerbating individualism, practices based on spatial appropriation, mutual help, sharing resources, and reproduction of the social space are still traceable, evidencing inhabitants' attachment and care for their neighborhood. As one inhabitant who moved into one of these

16 There are exceptions, where some areas in Bucharest entered the spiral of stigmatization towards ghettoization due to overlapping social and ethnic exclusions, combined with a chronic lack of public support.

The open garage typology. Inhabitants turn garages into pantries, workshops, play and hobby areas—even opening small stores and service spaces, all which became social hubs and local community nodes.

neighborhoods since its construction reflected on their evolution:

> "We all moved in the same time in the block, and we knew each other, you know, when you are there from the beginning the relation is different. Now it's more difficult; because many elderly moved away, to their children, or sold their apartments, and new tenants came in, and the block doesn't look like it used to be. But what is left now I say it's ok. It's still ok! I always liked the neighborhood."[17]

DRUMUL TABEREI: AN INHABITED UTOPIA

The Drumul Taberei neighborhood is one of the pinnacles of collective living in Romania. It was designed as an 'ideal city,' with generous public spaces and green areas. Even though the application of urban planning was incomplete, it greatly exceeded the pre-WWII and post-1989 revolution local achievements, providing an especially more equitable life to its inhabitants. At the same time, many of the neighborhood's premises

17 Excerpt from unpublished interviews realized by the author (Alex Axinte) as part of case study research initiated for their Ph.D. at the Sheffield School of Architecture (SSoA), University of Sheffield.

have not yet been fully actualized by subsequent actions. The neighborhood has always been an unfinished place, thus fertile for ad-hoc adaptations. As in most large collective housing neighborhoods, the dwellers developed a series of micro-interventions of negotiating and managing common spaces through collective care and repair practices. The survival of the framework derived from the attempt to materialize utopia and the soft practices developed by the inhabitants attached to their neighborhood are both represented in Drumul Taberei. Therefore, the neighborhood qualified as an ideal case study to understand a post-socialist city's operating mechanisms to articulate qualitative regeneration processes.

RESEARCH AND ACTIVATION

In this context, on the ground floor of a block of flats in the Drumul Taberei, in a former garage, former herbalist shop, and former tailor's shop, the OPEN Garage aimed to be an "extra room" for the inhabitants and

Libraries by the block. From the 1960 to the 1980s, numerous library branches were opened at the ground floor of newly constructed apartment buildings in the large collective housing neighborhoods. So-called 'libraries by the block' became the main typology of the network.

active field researchers in Buclă (the Loop).[18] The Garage is a proposal for community equipment, opened in a neighborhood comprised of blocks of flats. The project was developed through cultural activation, applied education, and action-based research. Located at street level, the Garage has triggered and supported research on the manifestation of informal collective practices of transforming and managing common spaces in the neighborhood while adapting its programming of cultural and educational activities according to the area's dynamics. The field research operated through a quantitative inventory documenting approximately 400 examples of spatial practices detected in the Garage's surrounding area, in combination with a series of qualitative methods, including (non-)participative observation, semi-structured interviews, collecting objects, and relational mapping. The research products included a Map of Collective Practices, and a laboratory exhibition opened in the Garage. The exhibition contained extracts

18 *Buclă*, the Loop, in English, is the nickname given by locals to the micro-rayon 7 area of the Drumul Taberei neighborhood in Bucharest due to its curved path.

from the research, with objects, photographs, installations, and artworks. In addition, a series of videos documented the initial project, illustrating several case studies with spatial transformations and informal uses by neighborhood' inhabitants. Furthermore, the Garage space and its nearby public spaces hosted a wide range of activities, from DIY, storytelling, or mapping workshops, to applied education for students from anthropology and landscape. But it all started with a library.

GARAGE LIBRARY: SHARING CULTURAL COMMON GOODS

With modest beginnings, almost fifty popular libraries were opened in Bucharest starting in the 1950s, especially in peripheral neighborhoods.[19] The need for urgent access and a constant lack of funds meant that houses

19 During the 1930s, Bucharest accounted for few public libraries, some limited to professional members only, according to Bucharest Statistic Register 1931-1936 and in Gh. Buluta, *Scurta Istorie a Bibliotecilor Din România* (București: Editura Enciclopedica, 2000). The ancestor of today's library network, the Municipal Library was opened in 1934, becoming truly public only in 1940, when it was properly housed, staffed, supplied, and easily accessible to the general public. For more on this, please see Pericle Martinescu, "Începuturi Modeste," in *Biblioteca Bucureștilor* I, no. 7 (1998): 15–16. The count of libraries is from the Bucharest Statistic Register for 1962.

of culture, workers' clubs, and especially nationalized buildings hosted them,[20] without any new constructions built as libraries. Following Soviet examples, the library system also grew in complexity and creativity. A diffuse network flourished beside the neighborhood branches through a series of mobile libraries, such as the *bibliobuz* (library in buses), temporary *summer libraries* (park libraries), pop-up *reading corners* (in factories), and even *home libraries* (home service) curated by individual residents for nearby communities. Following large-scale urban operations of the 1960 and 1970s, many library branches were relocated to ground floor spaces of newly built apartment blocks, becoming critical civic equipment in the collective housing estates, constantly under-serviced with public facilities.

Emerging from the pre-1989 context, when libraries mattered in society as, among the few keepers of common cultural goods, readers became attached to the library, developing a sort of loyalty, especially to their

20 Gheorghe Buluta, *Civilizația Bibliotecilor* (București: Editura Enciclopedica, 1998).

librarian, weaving a social network of library friends. This relational work enacted implicit community hubs embodied in everyday acts, like small exchanges, gestures of care and trust, mutual support, and sharing responsibilities. As one librarian remembers the early 1990s readers' attachment to the library:

> "I think these people came because they enjoyed being together, that we were all there at the library and that we felt we belonged to a family that helped each other when in need. (...) The library functioned as a community center, meaning people felt at home there."[21]

In the 1990s, austerity measures and the public grid's deconstruction affected the libraries too: in the past thirty years, all of their mobile programs have been canceled, and 30% of their spaces in the city were lost. Despite grim prospects, the, libraries adapted, survived, and even thrived, with librarians playing a central part. From roles close to their job description, like cultural facilitator or pedagogic disseminator, librarians expanded their skills and reached

21 Excerpt from page 17 of unpublished interviews realized by the author (Alex Axinte) in 2021 as part of case study research initiated for their Ph.D. at the Sheffield School of Architecture (SSoA), University of Sheffield.

out to their readers' needs for social interaction and personalized relations. Thus, recommending books in tune with readers' interests and moods while becoming trusted advisors, confidants, and even close friends, librarians acted as informal social workers and community agents, transforming their libraries into a relational device for locals beyond book exchange. The spatial and infrastructural resources of the library, together with their skilled relational librarians, supported activities excluded elsewhere, especially in the collective housing neighborhoods, where they helped to maintain small communities of proximity.

However, the constant closures of the libraries left vast parts of the city underserviced. Moreover, the only two small libraries in the Drumul Taberei neighborhood don't meet the required legal provisions.[22] In this context, the book exchange was one of the first programs tested at the OPEN Garage. The goals

22 According to the Libraries' Law no.334/2002, the existing libraries in Drumul Taberei cover about 6% of the legally required library area for its 300,000 inhabitants.

Informal practices. Transforming, using and managing common spaces assembled garden furniture, materializing the need—that became acute during the pandemic—for spaces of social interaction, through the creative and collective reuse of limited resources.

of the informal Garage Library were twofold: first, to advocate, even on an extra-small scale, for 1:1 solutions for the libraries' shrinkage in the city, and second, to participate somehow in the neighborhood network through a relational device. The library was also inspired by the historical "home libraries" program, which involved volunteers taking charge of library branches' small collections of books and further distributing them from their homes to their neighbors. As a result, the Library grew at the beginning as a collection for children and youth, with personal contributions, donations from neighbors or authors living nearby, and even new prints from the Arthur Publishing House. Furthermore, the Garage Library hosted activities and invited children attending the Library to join a series of educational and DIY workshops. As one parent testified in a radio interview about the actions in the Garage:

> "I liked it. I thought is something new, there were activities for kids, workshops. Most garages are just for parking and somehow with no future. No one

really comes to do something with them. I don't like them to remain so ugly."[23]

The Library evolved by working on trust and encouraging the readers' participation. Locals borrowed but also contributed, donated, and joined other activities. While spreading the word, they invited friends and neighbors or just passed by to say hello, creating a social space based on the book exchange. The everyday practice as an informal librarian at the Garage softened my position as an outsider. Being slowly included in neighborly rituals, like borrowing when in need, being included in local gossip, and participating in small exchanges based on care and trust, I moved from being an intruding researcher to becoming an accepted neighbor. The Garage space and its activities worked as a relational device between users and neighbors, making new connections and expanding existing ones, evidencing the potential of shared cultural goods to support the emergence of commoning practices.

23 Excerpt from unpublished interviews realized in the research phase of the OPEN Garage project in 2021.

GARAGES IN THE LOOP: EXTRA ROOMS

Perhaps owning a car was *the* dream project of the socialist emerging middle class, along with moving into a modern apartment block. Although housing became more accessible for large sections of the population, driving a car was still less accessible due to its scarcity and price. By the beginning of the 1970s, owning a car would spark a new function associated with collective living: the garages. The emerging middle class's need for comfort and their increased financial possibilities, combined with economic growth, doubled by the progress of prefabrication and facilitated by the architects' design tackling intimacy issues for the ground floor living while expanding apartments' storage spaces, made the garages possible. As the economic crisis set towards the end of the '70s, garages disappeared from the ground level of newly designed blocks. However, the need for extra storage didn't disappear, and the already built garages proved valuable spaces for their owners.

Before 1989, the number of private cars was small. Nevertheless, the urban planning and architectural design of the collective housing neighborhoods of the time were quite generous with the garages. Approximately 15% of the apartment blocks from the Loop have garages on the ground floor, while a standard block has 54 garages per 60 apartments. Most of their owners didn't have a car or were waiting for their long-placed order, so many of the garages became an "extra room." As five by three-meter spaces supplied with water, electricity, and heat, the garages became workshops, pantries, and places to meet, relax, or play. A resident shared their memories of the Loop garages of the 1970s to 1990s:

> "I find these spaces extremely versatile. You can do a lot in a garage like this, things you can't do in an apartment. In an apartment, if you have a bedroom, you have to sleep in it and that's all. Maybe you can have friends over. But in a garage, imagination is free to fly."[24]

24 Excerpt from page 23 of unpublished interviews realized by the author (Alex Axinte) in 2021 as part of case study research initiated for their Ph.D. at the Sheffield School of Architecture (SSoA), University of Sheffield.

After 1989, the garages saw improvements such as floor tiles, double-glazed windows, and plaster boarding. Eventually, they were sold and rented separately from the apartments on the real estate market. Their transformation also included extensions, like canopies which often marked the entrance of the small commercial and service-providing spaces.[25]

While mapping garages in the Loop, a few typologies emerged: *open garages* (commercial and services) with grocery, fruit-and-vegetable stores, wine shops, car parts, sanitary wares, as well as tailors and cobblers' workshops, barber shops, or vet and optician practices; *semi-open garages* (closed-circuit) used by friends and acquaintances to meet, socialize, have a barbecue and a beer together or for private classes for pupils, guitar lessons or DJ sessions; *closed garages* (private) used as the apartments' domestic extensions, storing furniture, sports gear, bicycles, pickles, canned fruit, jam, or as DIY workshops, gyms or play areas. The

25 Mihaela Staicu, *Amprente...: o incursiune antropologică asupra locuirii din marile ansambluri. Cazul Drumul Taberei* (București: Editura Universitară "Ion Mincu", 2013).

outside spaces in front of the garages became an extension of the garage's function. The open garages, which account for less than 5% of all the garages in Buclă, use the outside space for advertising, displaying goods, or meeting.
In front of semi-open or closed garages, locals also practice 'going out to the garage' as a form of relaxation and interaction with neighbors, taking part with their bodies in the life of the street. An older woman who is the owner of a garage converted into a small groceries store and meeting place for neighbors shared:

> "Given the age, it's very convenient. I discuss, I watch, I accumulate. I see the good and the bad. It keeps your mind awake."[26]

The interior and exterior repurposing of garages have turned some of them into informal social hubs, addressing the need for such spaces in the neighborhood, especially acute during the lockdown. However, the close vicinity to the apartments' windows in connection with an intensive commercial or social use

26 Excerpt from page 23 of unpublished interviews realized by the author (Alex Axinte) in 2021 as part of case study research initiated for their Ph.D. at the Sheffield School of Architecture (SSoA), University of Sheffield.

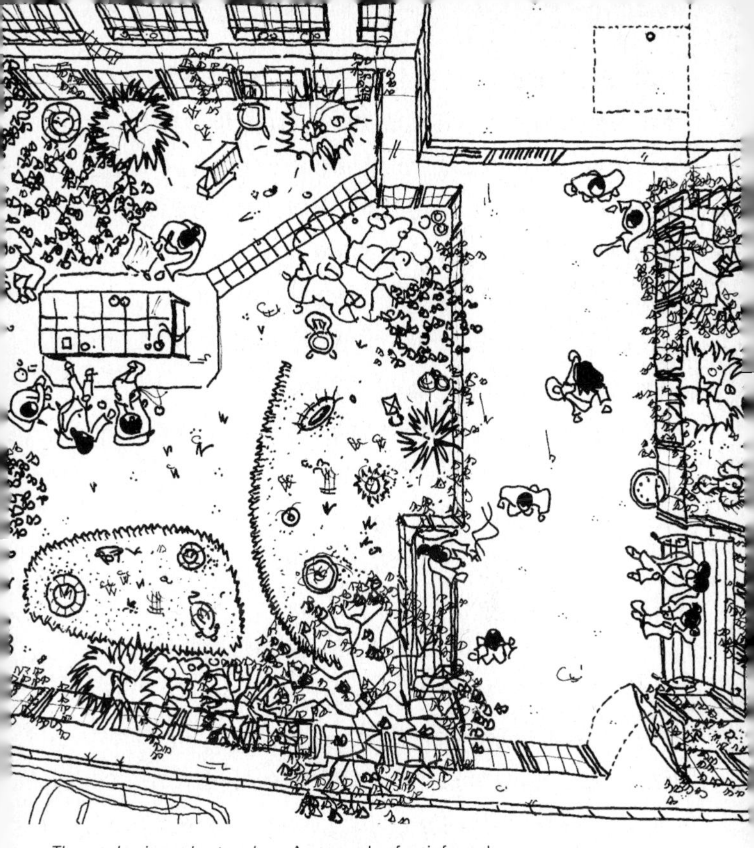

The pandemic garden typology. An example of an informal garden initiated and collectively managed by a group of neighbors developed from the showcase garden typology and featuring DIY beautification installations alongside infrastructure for relaxation and socialization of the garages, over a background of legal ambiguities can sometimes lead to disputes among suspicious neighbors. With conflict looming behind half-closed doors, garage goers and users are walking a thin line between solidarity and antagonism. It's not just garages that act as "narrative spaces" and opportunities for the socialization of proximity and DIY[27]. Green spaces between the blocks of flats have turned into social, informal gardens.

GARDENS IN THE LOOP: COURTYARDS BY THE BLOCK

Before 1989, maintaining the blocks' courtyards and their green spaces was the inhabitants' responsibility, and it was done through volunteer and collective actions organized by the tenants' associations.[28] Some inhabitants kept mixed feelings about the rather compulsory character of these actions. In contrast, others recollect these moments more as an occasion for socialization and

27 Richard Sennett, *The Conscience of the Eye: The Design and Social Life of Cities* (New York: W. W. Norton & Company, 1992).

28 According to the Streets Law, no.37/1975.

participation, of being with others, while carrying for their neighborhood spaces. Since then, gardening by the block has become a widespread and accepted practice, with a history dating back to the construction of the big collective estates. Gardening benefitted from access to resources, institutional support, and skilled inhabitants. As an individual or a collective practice, gardening was a form of relaxation and socialization for the newly housed working class. In response to the economic crisis and the food scarcity of the 1980s, a more productive form of gardens with vegetables and fruits was legally encouraged.[29] Beyond informal gardens by the blocks, the state allowed the unused public land in the neighborhood to be divided into small plots and planted by the locals, triggering the coagulation of genuine communities of neighbor-gardeners, as one inhabitant recalls growing up among the plot gardens of the 1970s to the 1990s in the Loop area:

29 According to the Supply Law, no.13/1980.

> "It was like a small community here, although we were from different blocks. Everyone was sharing. (...) All day we were: "Where are you going? To the garden!" It was like a kind of courtyard by the block, it was our space of freedom, of play, of anything."[30]

Despite dominant narratives pointing to aesthetic incoherence or legal requirements, communities of neighbor-gardeners triggered by diverse motivations keep emerging. The gardeners are not just retired residents but also diverse and active adults passionate about plants, crafts, and ecology. Today's gardens are based on the historical legacy of the practice of using contemporary resources, such as the internet and DIY stores. The arrangements result from individual projects or initiatives of several neighbors who collectively manage common spaces and shared resources.

Mapping Buclă's informal gardens by the block, several typologies arise: *the showcase garden* (arranging the green) with upcycling decorations, animal shelters, and flowers; *the*

30 Excerpt from page 23 of unpublished interviews realized by the author (Alex Axinte) in 2021 as part of case study research initiated for their Ph.D. at the Sheffield School of Architecture (SSoA), University of Sheffield.

Care and repair. In the face of the initial characteristics of the neighborhood's apartment blocks that included strict planning, generous access to resources, standardization and prefabrication, the residents moved in and appropriated the living spaces through tactics of care and repair.

talking-playing garden (activities in the green) with tables and benches by the shade and play elements for kids; *the planted garden* (working the green) with many flowers and shrubs, rarely with vegetables or fruits. Due to recent restrictions during the pandemic, like closed playgrounds or unemployment, the *pandemic garden* emerged and became permanent as a combination of several typologies. As one member of a collective of neighbor-gardeners from Buclă recalls the beginnings of their DIY garden:

> "The garden was actually unworked. The ground was dry, like concrete. And slowly we started. It was like a game at the beginning, but it worked. Everyone liked it. Many passers-by took pictures, congratulate us. It was investment, it was work. I think about 10% of the tenants participated both materially and with work."[31]

The research by the Garage evidenced how the collective practices for managing common spaces, like informal gardening, are both a manifestation and a source for inhabitants'

31 Excerpt from page 23 of unpublished interviews realized by the author (Alex Axinte) in 2021 as part of case study research initiated for their Ph.D. at the Sheffield School of Architecture (SSoA), University of Sheffield.

attachment to their neighborhood. Based on collaboration and solidarity, these practices were crystalized over time and became a way of being in the neighborhood for some inhabitants. By training locals to collaborate and organize, or by allowing socialization of proximity while supporting mental health and acting as spaces for practicing ecological skills and acquiring knowledge, gardening by the block stands as a valuable material and immaterial resource for the neighborhood and the local community. However, the less explicit governance model of sharing the space of the garden by the block sometimes leads to abuses and further conflicts among neighbors, as gardens can become private spaces, fenced off against destruction or theft, but also closed for other users except a select few. Nevertheless, gardens and the gardening practice were validated during the pandemic, when the need for socialization, solidarity, DIY, or caring about something could take shape in the proximity of the apartment block. Thus, attachment to the neighborhood and the

Care for others. Within the informal practice of gardening, taking care of animals intensified during the lockdown and was spatialized by the inhabitants of the neighborhood in different specific designs: from shelters, to feeders and to structures supporting their traffic from the garden to the flat and back.

community becomes a relational practice with a spatial manifestation.

In a Bucharest characterized by an exacerbated individualism, radical privatization, constant seizing, and closing of community spaces, these latent, implicit spatial practices of commoning are a form of immaterial heritage. The case study of the Drumul Taberei neighborhood and the research and activation of the OPEN Garage project illustrates 'nestedness' as an essential condition for the existence of urban commons. The fragmented grid in need of repair, maintenance, and support which triggers collaboration and care among its users, evidences the 'latent' commons in society.[32] In the post-socialist city, this latent commoning is a situated characteristic of the urban commons. Compelled by basic needs and urgent demands, growing from existing patterns of living together, determined by spatial and institutional local conditions, urban commons in the post-socialist city manifests more in the form of silent rituals for being together

32 Ibid, 2.

in the neighborhood than as an explicit and organized commoning.

Valuing and supporting commoning practices can be difficult in a context where commoning values were abused under dictatorship and further depreciated by the anti-communist narrative that dominated the post-socialist period. Articulating commons is equally challenging as even the language associated with 'collective,' 'solidarity,' or 'common' is historically loaded and contentious. Threatened by local administration's 'civilizing' perspectives which exclude informal contributions to the design and use of the in-between spaces, these practices also lack clear, explicit frameworks, exposing them to disputes and abuses. Thus, conflict often accompanies collaboration in and against the commoning process.

Nevertheless, research-driven projects like OPEN Garage can collect fresh evidence, and they can join the public narrative that regards collective practices as situated answers to present urban crises. The valorization, the support, and the articulation of such practices constitute viable propositions for the situated and qualitative regeneration of collective housing neighborhoods at scale.

A NOTE FROM THE AUTHOR:
Some passages in this text, compressed and edited, are based on the article "OPEN Garage. An extra room in the Loop," for *Zeppelin* magazine 165 (Spring, 2022). The interpretations and conclusions in this text resume part of the collective assessment and reflections on field research results shared with the OPEN Garage project team, composed of Alex Axinte, Bogdan Iancu, Iris Şerban, Anca Niţă, Ileana Szasz, Diana Culescu, Ioana Tudora, and Ioana Irimciuc. The conceptual framing, field research direction, portions of the analysis, and conclusions in this paper are undertaken in the context of Alex Axinte's practice-based Ph.D., coordinated by Dr. Doina Petrescu (first supervisor) and Dr. Emma Cheatle (second super-visor) at the University of Sheffield (TUoS), Sheffield School of Architecture (SSoA).

COMMONS

A CONVERSATION WITH ALEXANDRA TROFIN

● 44° 45'N – 21° 13'E

Alexandra Trofin is the coordinator of BETA, the Timișoara Architecture Biennial, an organization that is part of the Order of Architects. Throughout the years, they have carried out several research and exhibition projects questioning the state of the practice, enabling different agents to enter the process of reviewing the architecture practice critically. BETA's work articulates a framework for mediation where administrators, architectural practitioners, and residents meet in dialogue, where they can discuss topics such as housing, responsibility, or the topic of this year's edition, *The City as a Common Good*. In the following interview, Alexandra generously walks us through their aims, concerns, and methods. Before this year's edition begins, we discuss our shared interests in how commonality can happen and unfold in a situated manner.

Dear Alexandra, as the coordinator of the BETA Biennial 2022, what are the topics you are looking to address through this, the fourth edition? And why?

AT The fourth edition of BETA is being developed under the title *The City as a Common Good*. It is a topic that concerns all residents, administrators, and professionals. Now is the right time to address this topic because Timișoara will also be the Capital of Culture in 2023, which complements the work we have been doing in public space while also focusing on community engagement. For us, the administration must be open to discussing how to integrate topics like active residency, open governance, and other programs that are part of the consolidation of the *commons*. The Biennial is a complex structure with the main exhibition playing a central role. This year it is curated by Davide Tommasso Ferrando and Daniel Tudor Munteanu. Through the exhibition, we aim to disclose the policies and regulations that shape the city as well as the apparatuses of administrative models that regulate our urban spaces. The exhibition presents a series of strategies that can be replicated locally, offering concrete tools for residents to claim their rights to the city.

What is the organizational structure of the BETA Biennial, and what are its main objectives?

AT BETA Biennial is the cultural branch of the Romanian Order of Architects. We are a territorial project dedicated exclusively to this biennial endeavor. The chief objective of the project is to reflect on residents' understanding of the built environment and contribute to broadening and addressing their perspectives on city-making processes. In this sense, we act as a platform for mediation, defining frameworks of collaboration between actors. The Banat region, where we are located, is a historical area that also used to be part of Serbia and Hungary; therefore, establishing connections between other institutions, even the names of such institutions, is crucial. We try to include them in our programs as this allows us to give broad and diverse perspectives on the themes we are addressing.

An important activity for this collaboration is the Beta Competition, in which we encourage emerging regional practices to exhibit their work and thinking. This initiative allows us to observe and gain insight into what is happening within spatial practices every two years.

These activities aim to map out the architecture and urban practice across various scales; it is a multilayered study that gathers comprehensive knowledge in the region and is essential to us as an organization because we can draw relevant conclusions about the practice.

Can you expand on the role of the BETA Biennial as a platform for the collaboration of different actors from architecture and design practice that tackles common topics in the local context?

AT For each edition, we attempt to address subjects that are relevant worldwide. However, then, we put them in a local context and see how they coincide with local interests and specificities. In the previous edition, we worked on the theme of 'Responsibility': the responsibility we have as architects to re-think the built environment and the administration or residents' responsibility in a context of crisis. We strive to articulate powerful, optimistic, and forward-thinking discourses. We believe it is essential to focus on narratives that can create alternatives through propositions and imaginations rather than merely criticisms. Thus, promoting projects with a responsible and sustainable approach to resource usage, community engagement, and developing visions for fairer futures.

But I also do not want to be naïve. Currently, the practices that foster such a responsible perspective in Romania are still in the minority. However, I think it is important for us to acknowledge and disseminate their work so that they can serve as models and create a network of actors. For this edition, we are digging into topics like 'commons' or 'open city' to advance the evolution of

this line of thinking. We gather small and medium-sized practices to exemplify and inform us about the possibilities of acting differently.

In terms of discourses, what are the main challenges of mainstream spatial practice in Romania?

AT What I will say comes mainly from my observations, even if my experience as a practitioner in the Romanian architectural context is short. During that time, I saw limited discourse and that architectural and urban practice is rather chaotic and often based on liberal developments. Everybody is moving forward but without coordination. BETA is attempting to help fill this gap by contributing to a broader discourse and composing a framework in which we can collectively do things better. For example, the new regulations from the New Green Deal are helping to transform the ways in which the built environment is being produced in Romania. But we still need to land these proposals at the local level and make decisions that contribute to improving urbanity in the long run.

Through Radical Rituals, we question notions of center and periphery in Europe. However, we also don't want to be naïve as we recognize that, from a cultural point of view, there is indeed often a central narrative and a peripheral one. Your work holds the potential to inform local contexts, but it is also eye-opening for so-called central perspectives. How do you see this relation between narratives?

AT I don't think we are at the periphery—we are not even discursive. We address topics of central importance regarding our day-to-day concerns—regionally and worldwide. Living in Romania can be as expensive as in any other place in Europe. However, here the problem is about quality. The standard of services is often poor, which is interesting to us. We want to present spatial examples of high quality in terms of resource management and social engagement to improve the overall level of design practice in the region. The exhibition of 2020 presented many adequate practices working on how to build differently. These practices can serve as examples for alternative protocols and better outcomes.

This year you are approaching the topic of ′common goods′; this is also a matter relevant to our investigation along the 45°N parallel, for it includes the disclosure of methods and practices of design. How do you describe the concept of 'commons' in the development of this edition of the Biennial?

AT From the very beginning, when we decided to start working with the *commons*, we acknowledged the problem of the term in this region. We, however, think it is time to discuss it and face the contradictions instead of avoiding the topic. It is a legacy from the communist period, and it is sometimes a limitation. Commons means so much more than our historic communist background, so it is important to take apart the topic and expand into its possibilities. This year, commons is a matter of shared resources, specifically in the urban space. Public space comes closest to the main tangible form of commons that we are familiar with in our physical surroundings: any one of us can use it and understand how it functions.

We address the topic of commons from several perspectives. For example, the exhibition has a provocative approach, presenting different examples of how people actively take agency in their spatial surroundings. We present subjects and examples to provide tools for people to replicate actions. At the same time, we also take a more formal approach with the administrations and the architecture profession, creating a connection between their needs. Together we aim to make the legislation on the use of public space more straightforward and comprehensive for the wider public to enhance and expand the possibilities of the uses of public space. Furthermore, we inform residents about the potential uses of the city and try to enable an educational dialogue with both institutions and residents. Accordingly, we have two approaches: one consists of direct examples of hands-on projects, and the other approach entails the deeper work of knowledge-sharing with the institution.

We want to disclose the procedures that frame the city because it is currently an indeterminate territory. For example, if you want to close off a street for activity and occupy a public space, you are often unaware of your rights and the possibilities and steps you can follow. Together with the administration, we want to map out and make accessible the protocols that any resident may follow in order to have free access to the space. This process of disseminating knowledge must be through a shared, comprehensive language and a wide range of formats like newspapers, open-source guides, workshops, etc. We believe our mediating role is fundamental in this process and leads to major forward steps in making a more open city.

How is this role of mediation defined in the context of the Biennial so that it reaches a broad audience and is not limited to a disciplinary public?

AT In the context of BETA 2018, which focused on housing, mediation and vocabulary were of great importance to us. We were undergoing a real estate boom where everyone was buying houses. The BETA team created a guide called *Ghid practic pentru cei care caută un apartament* (Practical Guide for Those Looking for an Apartment) to inform people of the steps they need to follow when buying an apartment. Buying a property is a huge step; it significantly affects people's lives, and the quality of facilities must correspond to the amount of money they invest. Therefore, we created a guide that is accessible to the public to understand what technical and spatial aspects they have to pay attention to, such as the location, legal bases, regulatory standards, and the quality of the materials. The guide is a comprehensive, accessible overview of protocols and uncovers previously hidden information about the housing market. We couldn't stop the prolific real estate market development back then. Still, we could contribute to generating a critical public that asked for the right standards, thus ultimately affecting the overall quality of new dwellings.

Do you notice a paradigm shift or an emergence of practices in Romania and around Europe that blur disciplinary boundaries? And why might this be of interest to BETA?

AT There is a worldwide paradigm shift in architecture practices. Nevertheless, I do not think it is a sudden shift

but a compendium of actions that naturally has grown all over from the economic and social crisis. Architects are changing their roles in societies beyond the conventional ones; we could talk about a professional adaptation to new conditions. We have become problem-solvers, from identifying to proposing and executing alternatives. In this context, the role of BETA is to observe, analyze and document this shift and its complex threads; this cultural project was built slowly throughout many years in Timișoara—even before BETA. Nevertheless, the discourses have been shifting, and we can undoubtedly illustrate this thread to see its evolution. All of this encourages us to keep on doing what we are doing.

How do you see the future of the built environment in this regional context? And how do you envision BETA as a platform for reflection upon spatial practice?

AT I wish to consider our profession's impacts on our planet and societies. To do this, we must work on developing and strengthening our listening, carefully bringing diverse perspectives together. In this context of crisis and conflict, we need to be conscious of the changes our surroundings are undergoing and use our knowledge to respond in the best way. Perhaps the role of BETA aims to contribute to visions on what to do next or how to do it differently. I don't think we can change the world, but we can contribute to a new world with our community, professionals, and skills. In the end, a big part of the shift is to have access to good examples and references to learn from. Therefore, our most considerable effort must be towards identifying the necessities of architects, administrations, and civil society. Although their needs and requirements are broad and complex, they are also precise. It is up to us to find them and bring them to the table to try and negotiate until we can come to an agreement.

STAȚIA EXPERIMENTALĂ DE CERCETARE PENTRU ARTĂ ȘI VIAȚĂ

● 44° 45'N – 26° 10'E

We met with Raluca Voinea in the city center of Bucharest. Together, we drove about an hour outside of the urban landscape to reach the place where the group started their new project, Stația Experimentală de Cercetare pentru Artă și Viață (The Experimental Research Station for Art and Life). We arrived in a field that, until recently, was cultivated with wheat. While we watched the neighboring field of sunflowers being harvested, Raluca explained how, in recent years, her practice has shifted to being more concerned with agriculture than culture.

Raluca Voinea's work as curator and writer focuses on the relations between humans and nature—*nature-culture*—and, although both are intrinsically connected, her interests are now more connected to life. She was compelled to become a foundational part of the team for a project where theory and practice could meet and merge: Stația de Cercetare. Raluca has been co-running the independent institution for contemporary art, Tranzit.ro, which is part of the more extensive regional network Tranzit.org that is present in Austria, Czech Republic, Slovakia, Hungary, and Romania. The platform has existed in Eastern Europe for twenty years and in Romania for almost ten years, where it operates in four cities: Cluj, București (Bucharest), Iași, and Sibiu. Each location has self-initiated projects, but they work collaboratively as one national institution, sharing many principles and lines of work. The network has a coordinated agenda balanced between two organizational levels; the international one functions as a support structure for the local and national ones, which can maintain autonomy and independent programs.

For over seven years, Tranzit.ro was running a space in the south of Bucharest. The space was a unique place, not a conventional art space or gallery, but instead consisting of two main projects: one exhibition space and one smaller space, the Orangery, for informal events and gatherings. The place had a garden that naturally evolved as the heart of Tranzit.ro, shaping, over time, its core identity. The garden became strongly connected to the art projects and, together with other informal platforms, a community formed. Projects grew in close observation and relation to the environments and the natural landscapes around them. Thus, developing a curatorial perspective around the topics like nature-culture, food sovereignty, and climate change were addressed. Unfortunately, the space and the garden closed in 2019 because of high rent and costly maintenance: "The most difficult thing was," Raluca told us, "to leave that garden and all the projects we created around it, including the community that grew over time, organically, mixing professional and personal relationships." After the closure amid the pandemic, the Tranzit community began a process of revising its goals and activities. The team saw this event as an incentive to radically rethink their mission as art and cultural practitioners.

In the Romanian context, artist-run platforms and initiatives usually exist for just three years or less. And so, "rather than moving from one precarious scenario to the next, we took this opportunity to think deeply about how to become self-sustainable and independent," Raluca shared. However, since sustainability is connected to economic sustenance, the team realized that the operation was only possible if they moved out of Bucharest. Hence,

Raluca proposed to artists and other cultural practitioners connected to the community that they could buy land and build something similar to what they had in Bucharest, but on a different scale and, more importantly, permanently. On their decision-making process, Raluca Voinea shared:

> "If the Tranzit Association builds a long-term structure, its survival will be less dependent on its ability to pay rent from external funding. This capacity is essential as getting funding in Romania is very challenging, and cultural institutions cannot often be self-sustainable. In the case of the withdrawal of main funding foundations, cultural projects and art spaces are frequently unable to continue."

Consequently, the group aimed to grow on a long-term basis with a sustainable financial model. For Tranzit, it was essential to break the precarious pattern, so they decided, in the context of the pandemic and crisis, to allow themselves the space to imagine and build a collective project on their terms. This imagining of the future and shape of the space began with a collective design process. In seeking to create a structure that could survive through time, the idea of buying a space arose. Tranzit had to overcome the old, familiar means of cultural production by recognizing their agency to make independent decisions. This fundamental acknowledgment allowed them to concentrate on generating a creative context for artistic research that was not subordinate to hegemonic structures but instead creates and holds a safe context for exploring their true interests. Art production is a central part of their activities, so they address these activities in correspondence between the goals of the Station and their ways of living, both as individuals and as a community. This very principle brings another sense to the word *life*.

It was then that the team started understanding the effect of their community garden: it was not merely a side project but of primary importance to their practice. After contemplation and reflection, Tranzit prioritized research and reflection instead of just focusing on production. As a result, and in direct relation to the local typology of existing research bases, the group founded The Experimental Research Station for Art and Life questioning what a 'research station' could be.

Romania has many research stations that monitor and investigate life and the various conditions that enable or hinder it. There are many such stations, though they are primarily focused on agriculture. In many places, these stations are aging and obsolete time capsules; in some cases, however, the stations are able to conduct progressive, avant-garde research. In the south of Romania, for example, there is a station that researches desertification and plants that can grow in the sand because, in that area of the country, there is already a significant desert with dunes called the Sahara Olteniei (Oltenian Sahara).

By 2021, Tranzit bought land in Siliștea Snagovului, a village close to Lake Snagov and a one-hour drive from Bucharest. The Research Station consists of approximately sixteen people, including part of the Tranzit team alongside artists and colleagues from Bucharest. Many of the people involved in the Station live abroad; joining the Station meant joining the community, an anchor of

cultural production in Romania. Numerous collaborations have emerged between the members, all based on making the project sustainable through time. "Many of the artists involved here have an interest in plants, botany, natural sciences, and climate change," Raluca told us. "Therefore, because we have the chance to build this space from the ground, we need to directly build it through ecological principles." Often, institutions are able to develop a progressive program that explores these topics, but they cannot fully establish the programs in terms of ethics or resources. To Tranzit, it is crucial to try, as much as possible, to be sustainable in how they build and organize the project. Here theory and practice are encouraged to be reciprocal, nurturing each other.

In Romania, after the *Revoluția Română* (Romanian Revolution) of 1989, people tended to dismiss the idea of cooperative work. And although cooperation and collectivity have begun to resurface through art and culture, it is not yet strong enough to influence the mainstream cultural sector and beyond. The Tranzit network has existed for twenty-some years through mutual respect for each one's context, environment, and needs. In its imagining, the Station should operate and adhere closely to the idea of respecting local ways of living.

Raluca hopes that there will be more similar or complementary projects around the same area so that they can build together and consider the ecosystem surrounding them—both natural and cultural. For them, sustainable thinking refers to how one frames and conducts their relationships with others and nature, and being consistently coherent with those sustainable principles makes it possible to truly think in the long term. One such form of coherent cohabitation is to be site-specific. Raluca and Tranzit show us multiple ways exist to address an international spectrum of interests while being grounded in the local. Through this new research station, the entire team wants to make it possible for contemporary culture to serve as a model for flourishing practice and, in so doing, create a lasting legacy.

ASOCIAȚIA CULTURALĂ ȘI ECOLOGICĂ SEPALE

Silvia Moldovan

• 45° 22'N – 21° 42'E

In March 2017, a sanctuary for non-predatory birds, the SEPALE Cultural and Ecological Association, was conceived of and founded by Silvia Moldovan. A point of reception, a place to take care of birds, a shelter for disabled birds, a center for pigeons, and a park, SEPALE wants to be an alternative space for various cultural, artistic and educational events.

Currently, the SEPALE bird shelter operates in the outskirts of Timișoara, next to Calea Urseni. When we arrive, Silvia is waiting for us on the top of one of the shelters' roofs, perched among many resting birds. It is a space with several constructions, all of them singular and visually chaotic; the variety of objects and elements are meant to serve the various necessities of the different birds. Silvia walks us through the space, explaining the different uses, kinds of shelters, and facilities for different bird species. Throughout the conversation, we are mesmerized by the choreographies in the air—and Silvia's relationship with them.

"This is a very messy place. Working with animals can be chaotic, and everything is constantly under construction. Everybody talks about multi-species conviviality, but few will get their hands dirty," Silvia tells us while she crosses the main square of the shelter. Meanwhile, the flock of birds is constantly moving above our heads: they are exploring the edges of the built environment, and their bodies' choreographies shape an upper landscape unreachable to us. In the main square below, Silvia has gathered works from artists, including Bogdan Matei and Cosmin Haias. Over a thousand birds live in the shelter; they rest there, feed themselves, and socialize. Many spend the day elsewhere, though most birds return to the shelter during the evenings.

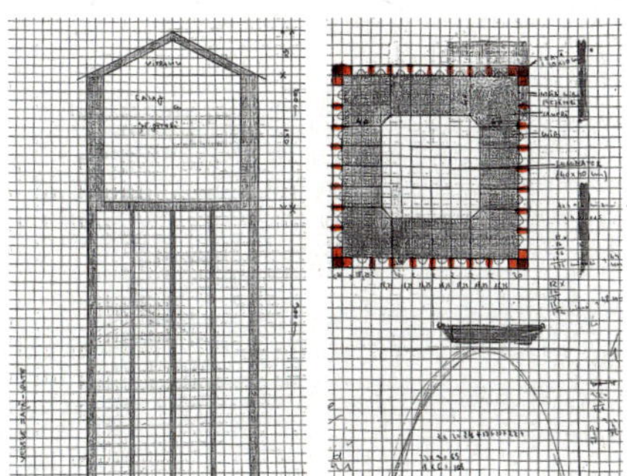

Silvia has been working on bird care since 2008. The shelter, voluntary work, occupies most of her time. Over the years, she has become an autodidact, seeking and gaining a vast knowledge of birds' behavioral patterns through her experience. She is now prototyping a city pigeon shelter, and when she shows us the sketches, there is an aesthetic genealogy evocative of John Hejduk.

Timișoara's local government has forbidden feeding pigeons in public spaces. In Silvia's appraisal, this recent measure is a perverse one: although there may be too many pigeons in the city, they still need care; if they are not well fed, they will become sick—many die. Instead of letting the pigeons starve to death, the city council should propose regulating the pigeon population through birth and medical control so they can have a healthy life. "Pigeons are not wild animals; humans domesticated them and brought them to the city," Silvia reminds us. "Now, the city is their natural environment; we are responsible for that." The pigeon city shelter also allows for bird and human interaction; it functions as urban furniture where pigeons can have clean water, eat, and rest. By now, SEPALE has submitted its project proposal and is looking for sponsorships to fund its project prototype. Silvia and SEPALE believe this could be a viable, meaningful alternative to restrictive animal laws, instead building and maintaining a healthy relationship with—and population of—pigeons in the city.

ATELIER AD HOC ARHITECTURA

Daria Maria Oancea and George Marinescu

● 44° 26'N – 26° 05'E

At a nineteenth-century family house turned co-working studio space in Bucharest, we meet George and Daria Maria. This typology has become common as there are no office buildings in the city center. Atelier Ad Hoc Arhitectura is an architecture practice that explores the familiarity and intimacy of living through design, seeking to understand the complexity of the built environment and finding creative, valuable, and specific solutions for each proposal. Their projects are carried out by two entities: a design studio and a non-governmental association. When we meet, they walk us through several of their projects that entangle practices on the threshold of commons, non-commodified uses of space, and the practice of architecture.

In 2020, Ad Hoc, in collaboration with MaiMultVerde, developed *Public Infrastructure for Cheson Beach* in the city of Zimnicea and its surrounding villages along the Danube river. The physical intervention was situated on one of the few public beaches on the river banks accessible to all village residents. It is a natural beach, but the public administration does not take care of its maintenance. To attract residents' interest in taking care of and enjoying this space, George and Daria Maria designed infrastructures for the community to use the space in diverse ways while promoting strategies for cleaning and caring for their surroundings. Thanks to its versatility, this linear wooden structure, accessible from the beach and the forest, interacts with different publics, ages, and interests. And now, unlike before, the maintenance of the natural beach and furniture is the responsibility of the neighboring community.

Another Ad Hoc project, *The Third Instance*, reflects the threshold between private and public in the domestic sphere. They studied spaces of diffuse ownership, looking at how people's relationship with property has changed over the past fifty years in Romania, from the communist period to the start of liberalism. They began by collecting the stories of people who transitioned from national public-owned housing (socialist housing) to private units, focusing mainly on daily living conditions. Several families, for example, frequently had to share housing units meant for a single household. This regulation produced forced co-living situations where the *thresholds* of corridors, bathrooms, and halls all became the public space. Facilities designed for single-household usage were collectivized; consequently, every door to a private room within the household became a property limit. In contrast, the rest of the house became a space of negotiation. The door, in this case, is a confine that defines the clear and diffuse ownership. To study this element, they designed a set of transformable doors, allowing it to become a set of foldable furniture, making it habitable. Doors can expand the limits of diffuse ownership and make it present.

A project that considered the political background of the country is the *Bucharest Dossier*, and Daria Maria and George explain to us how they studied survival practices in the city after the transition from Communism in the '90s. At that time, groups of people were excluded from the new structures shaped by capitalism, and as happened in many other cities, many were left behind and ended up living in the street. Over the last few decades, George and Maria have been researching how unhoused people use and produce urban situations and how they inhabit the cracks of the city, compelled to establish their own domestic spaces and non-commodified ways of living. The study gathered a set of typologies of so-called 'extended living' scenarios where their housing setting is scattered at the city level. After the research, when it comes to design, the strategy they followed used the perimeter of a homeless shelter in Bucharest as a prototype of a *threshold* that connected the inner and outer facilities. The aim was to directly upgrade the living conditions of residents by placing infrastructures within the limits of the shelter, making the extended living scenario visible. In addition, they sought to expand the accessibility of basic uses such as the possibilities for hygienic services and water supply, laundry, and storage, allowing hopeful users to use necessary facilities 24 hours a day without having to enter the shelter, which closes at night. Atelier Ad Hoc recognized these specific needs through their design approach and implemented them into the infrastructure.

These conflicting but complementary conceptions of commons in a post-communist context allow for the finding and making of spaces of diffused ownership by creating non-commodified activities and uses, enabling other ways of conviviality. Atelier Ad Hoc works with these intermediate spaces that are not completely private or public: they recognize that opportunities exist in the threshold to explore more diverse and inclusive needs and, accordingly, new possible uses. For Atelier Ad Hoc, experimentation in between is an ongoing learning process that continuously compels them to revise their practice, questioning their role as architects.

GRUPUL DE INIȚIATIVĂ CIVICĂ CIȘMIGIU

Matei David

● 44° 26'N – 26° 05'E

We met with Matei David in Grădina Cișmigiu (Cișmigiu Gardens), one of the few green public spaces in central Bucharest. Matei is part of the initiative Grupul de Inițiativă Civică Cișmigiu (Cișmigiu Civic Initiative Group) which has been active since 2016. It began as a community-building process, looking to engage the area's residents to respond to the diminished state of the park. Matei David told us: "It had deteriorated so that few residents, for years, would use this public space." The Cișmi Civic group got together to restore it, to bring it back to life and make it usable and enjoyable. In the beginning, the group planned a first action: cleaning an area and collectively painting a wall. As they began, a few people were painting together. As they started, people living in the area saw their efforts and joined. By the end of the day, many neighbors ended up working together, and the potential of generating a more cohesive project became obvious to the group.

In Romania, green spaces are state-owned. But the state is often unable to manage them; they become the black holes of cities, where public policies tend to invest a minimum effort into maintaining such areas. Cișmi Civic was the first group to use the park as a platform to leverage multiple interests instead of the more orthodox approach that focuses on a singular issue. Since Cișmi Civic's first project, diverse groups—anthropologists, architects, urban planners, and sociologists—have been compelled, through their varying interests, to develop a structure for the project. As an association, Cișmi Civic tries to connect people who are interested in specific subjects, such as ecology, animal care, and beekeeping, with specialists who can provide professional knowledge and training. Cișmi Civic began by analyzing neighbors' areas of interest and needs through questionnaires and interviews. Then, they used those results to successfully apply for a large grant to make the project feasible. They mapped out small and medium-sized green spaces between dwellings and coordinated and enabled groups to take responsibility for their care.

For Cișmi Civic, as a group driven to civic initiatives, it is crucial to share awareness and knowledge with the residential population so that they know how to take care of a garden: "The neighbors are generally eager to help take care of the garden because they use it on a daily basis. They just need the empowerment and knowledge to act on it." As a result of their efforts, the project has become a non-disciplinary educational space. When they connect residents and experts, each team develops a set of responsibilities over time. One successful example of these collaborations is the ornithologists working with bird species and sound pollution; they took samples from the park and analyzed how city noise affects birds' lives, producing a sound map. Other examples are Cișmi Civic's working with veterinarians, taking care of stray animals on the street, while a beehive on the top of a nearby building is cared for. A group of biologists and scientists study the city's pollution levels by analyzing the park's bees and their honey. Bucharest is an ideal environment for bees due to an extraordinary array of nectar and pollen in the urban and surrounding landscapes for the forager bees to collect and produce honey. The initiative continues to grow as Cișmi Civic is managing several community gardens along Strada Ion Brezoianu.

The group understands the garden as an ecosystem and their communitarian landscape strategy has become a knowledge-sharing platform, where everybody learns about caring for plants, biodiversity in urban contexts, the conservation of green public areas, and by extension, each other.

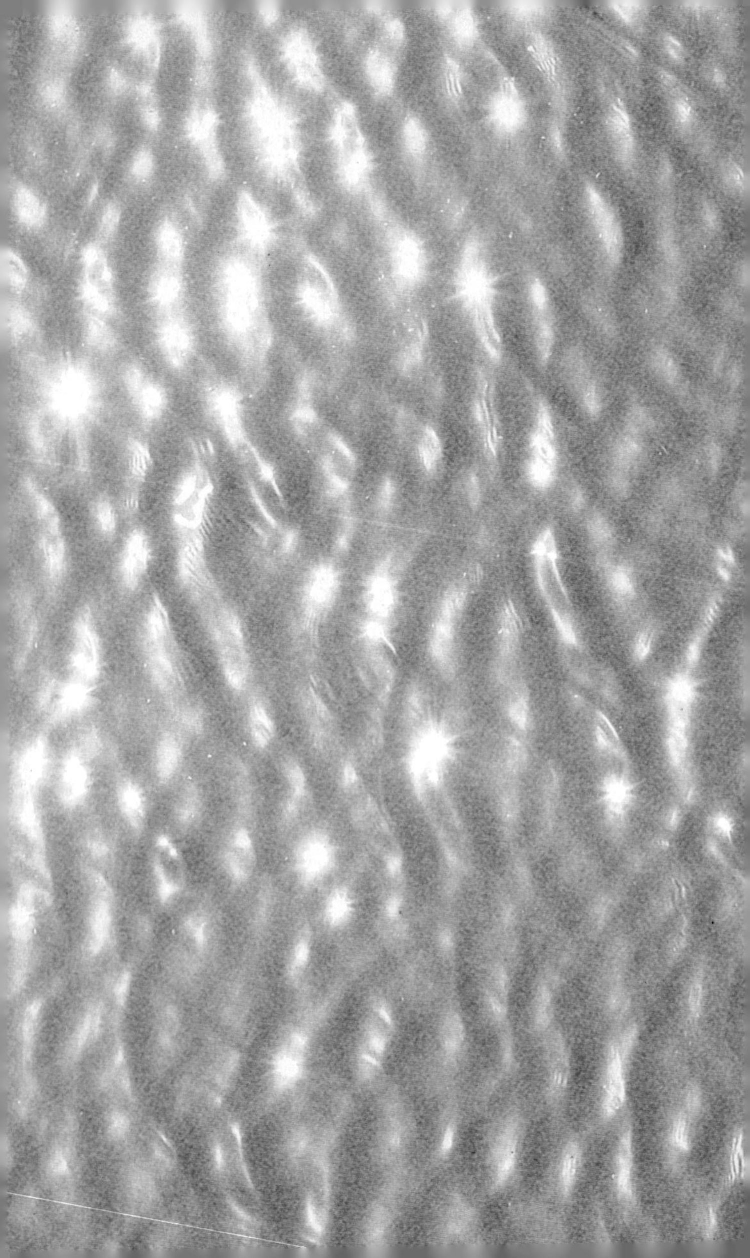

WATERS

A CONVERSATION WITH LOREDANA PANĂ

● 44° 13'N – 30° 10'E

During the last ten years, Loredana Pană has been working in Letea, a village in the midst of the Danube Delta. After the pandemic began, she moved her residency to Bucharest, where she is currently based. We met in a café in the middle of the city, close to Cișmigiu Park. Loredana Pană has spent almost twelve years working for non-governmental organizations (NGOs) that focus on social, humanitarian, cultural, educational, and environmental projects throughout the Danube Delta and Bucharest. Since 2015, she has worked for Ecopolis, an NGO based in Bucharest, but she frequently travels to the delta to carry out local projects. The socio-economic status of the Danube Delta is becoming more and more vulnerable by the year, despite its remarkable cultural and natural heritage. Loredana has involved herself in projects that aim to sustainably develop the region, primarily through empowering and training residents to identify alternative sources of income with a low environmental impact. In 2018, she started a project to transform a building owned by Ecopolis into a community center. We spoke with Loredana about the vernacular conditions of the region, the sense of time in an ever-changing landscape, and the relevance of enhancing the quality of life in the Danube Delta.

Dear Loredana, for over ten years, you have been working and living in the Danube Delta region, in Sulina. Can you tell us how you came to work in the Delta and where this interest of yours comes from?

LP The Danube Delta is a unique landscape and a UNESCO site. Unfortunately, people living in this area do so under precarious conditions; they are isolated because of the remoteness of some areas, and villages often have no accessible transportation over land. Furthermore, residents don't have access to education, healthcare, and other basic services daily. Their economies are fragile, products are expensive due to transportation costs, and there is a general lack of goods shipped to this region.

My first job was for an NGO called Save the Delta. The first project I developed with them focused on providing medical care to the remote villages of the Danube River. I was fascinated by witnessing how unusual it was for them to see a doctor. For some, it was their first time. After traveling around the area for a few weeks, I decided to continue working in the region; I realized my skills and perspectives coming from a city were valuable assets to be implemented in this particular context.

Over time, you have been delving deeper into the cultural and ecological heritage of the region. What is your approach to this legacy of the delta?

LP After my first experience at Save the Delta, I became fascinated by the natural and cultural richness of the Danube Delta. I decided to start working on environmental issues, cultural heritage, and community engagement by bringing together local resources while taking care of this captivating landscape. My focus has unfolded in several projects and several ways. For example, in 2015, we created the Delta Craft project, in which we generated and facilitated livelihoods for people without pressuring

the ecosystem. To do this, we contacted local craftsmen who use local techniques and traditional knowledge and brought them together to create products with Romanian designers. By now, we have gathered over twenty different products produced locally with vernacular craftwork and exhibited the products in Vienna, Bucharest, and other international settings. With this project, we want to emphasize not only the natural value of the Danube Delta but also its cultural and social value.

When we first contacted you during our preliminary research, our interest was spurred by the community house in Letea. This comprehensive project connects education, capacity building, community engagement, and heritage. How are you developing this educational project at the moment?

LP Letea is a good example of an isolated region in the delta with its picturesque setting, consisting of traditional housing and sand roads. A unique, raw settlement. It is unusual for any organization or administration to collaborate with the region for any development or financial support, so these regions tend to be suspended in time. In 2018, we decided to buy one house in Letea and renovate it using traditional, local techniques. When we arrived, the residents were excited! We collaborated with architecture students during an arts and crafts summer school, and the materials were based on local crafts, using reeds for the roof and mud for the walls. It was an intense learning process for everybody as knowledge and skills were shared across generations and geographies between people in and outside the village. I was impressed to see such wonderful teams coming together. I believe this collaboration added great value to our cultural heritage as it allows for the preservation and passing on of traditional knowledge and skills. At the moment, we are trying to set up a community center that can comply with resident's basic needs but also serve as a place to exchange with people from outside of the delta.

After living and working there for a long time, how has your relationship developed and unfolded with residents and local communities?

LP Relationships here take a lot of time and care before they can develop; people are not trusting of visitors. Our first strategies were to engage simply and to establish insights that were true to their cultures and backgrounds. Though it has been difficult to gain the trust of people who live here, now that the door has been opened, we can act like a bridge, bringing different people and knowledge together. Towards the beginning of my time here, we started a project with the women of the village to learn about and share their traditions and recipes. We started tracing a generational and cultural thread, talking about how, where, and from whom they learned their local dishes and where the ingredients came from. Besides this activity, we arranged for a gynecologist to come to do check-ups since they do not have regular access, with some having not seen a gynecologist for twenty years. This was a great success.

How do you see the role of the administration in its relationships with local communities? And how is the preservation of the natural reserve from the administrative and resident's perspective?

LP The infrastructure in the Danube Delta is often poor, and regulations are strict due to the natural reserve. This impacts how the population perceives the administration's role since their only contact is often negative, wherein the administration dictates and enforces rules but rarely provides resources or offers aid. For example, in many areas, fishing is their main economic activity. But fishing is also now forbidden without providing an alternative livelihood; regulations constrain possible ways of living. Another example is the transportation infrastructure, where all roads are sand, making daily commutes arduous.

In general, the relationship between residents and people outside of the delta, whether from the administration or visitors, is distant. They don't rely on other people so easily. But, as I mentioned previously, our relationship has been built over time, and even with me, after ten years, it is not always personal or even straightforward.

This detachment from administrative endeavors is reflected in many ways. Another example is the lack of a waste management system. There are poorly implemented waste protocols, and because of this, litter usually ends up in the water. With the Letea project, we decided to act upon this issue in two ways: a campaign and a design contest. For the contest, designers proposed several solutions for the design of trash bins adapted to the context of Letea, local necessities, and the landscape.

The area of Letea is becoming a tourist attraction for its unique surroundings and beautiful forest. However, tourists are often not so interested in understanding the

region's current situation: they come for a few hours and leave. Local people work seasonally, organizing a few tours with boats and cars, but this activity damages the biotope as the water gets contaminated and natural channels are destroyed. In the past, residents of the region used to be more careful; however, today, they do not feel as connected with their natural surroundings. We need to find a balance between the local economy and the ecosystem. But in the last few years, overfishing has been causing problems with the repopulation of the river. We need a balance that offers a better alternative to this precarious, seasonal economy in combination with protecting this vulnerable ecosystem. This is not a responsibility just for the region's inhabitants, but we must act collectively and provide the needed tools. Administrations should play a role in this process.

You have mentioned the historic confluence of cultures in the region and described the delta as a rugged landscape when it comes to its physical integration with the rest of the country. How is the Danube Delta perceived as a border?

LP There is great diversity in the Delta region. Over fifteen ethnicities in the Danube Delta have been living here peacefully for decades. It is a unique place in Europe. Its materiality, shaped by exchanges between land and water, brings about ethereal conditions, making it mercurial and mystic. There are a lot of stories about mermaids and holy spirits that inhabitants here have carried through their legacies. When we arrived, we wanted to understand what was 'traditional' and 'local' to those who lived here, and what we saw was a richness and mixed cultures. We noticed that, somehow, many objects acquired have a compact or transportable condition in order to endure. Unlike the mountains where everything is rocky and woody, here, everything changes, disappearing from time to time. Because of this, symbolic objects are often small, and belongings are few. They know how to appreciate nature and its force, the past, and the loss of life to live with constant changes. Here, there are many floods, people die, and things are not solid. In some way, this fluidity shapes their character and means of living. I never saw these conditions from the perspective of a border. But of course, the sense of belonging here is altered, perhaps shaped by bordering conditions. Thus, not only political but physical and natural.

The Danube Delta is a culturally rich and diverse region where many ethnic groups have settled for years. I think it is important to understand what their power is—and to invest the resources needed to enhance it. With these projects, we started to engage the local community in many small steps to ground the basis for preserving natural and cultural heritage.

To end our conversation, we would like to look to the near future. During the lockdown in 2020, you moved your residency to Bucharest. What are your plans for the delta? Are you planning to return?

LP During the pandemic, we paused the project and moved out of the area. We did not want to expose people to COVID-19 because medical treatment there is often inaccessible, and the population comprises many elderly people. Though the number of cases was low and stable, we did not want to increase them. We are currently applying for funding to continue the project because we don't have the resources to move there again.

In the future, we would like to fund a summer school for children to teach them non-curricular topics such as crafts, design, biodiversity, and English. Our main goal is to create conditions that preserve both the natural and cultural heritage in order to develop the area and its residents in a sustainable way. I developed a deep bond with this landscape and its people. I hope to find a way to come back to the delta very soon.

SOMEȘ DELIVERY

● 46° 46'N – 23° 35'E

We met with Silviu Medeșan, from the initiative Casa Verde (Green House), in the city center of Cluj-Napoca. Together we took a bus to the city's outskirts, to a neighborhood called Florești. There, a group of architecture students is building several installations along the banks of the river Someş. This initiative is called Someș Delivery, a series of events led by a non-governmental organization called MiniMASS and formed by architects, cultural practitioners, and students to protect Romanian waters and revindicate access to the public rivers. The event-based pedagogic program visualizes the multiple water management problems while creating learning and community-building places. Since 2015, they have been temporarily occupying the river banks from the city center with their installations. In their last edition, they decided to move to the periphery, enlarging the project's scope and revealing the river's hidden public areas.

Florești is a peculiar neighborhood that exhibits the complexity of Romanian land regulations in which private plots are being rapidly developed without the guise of a general planning framework. This uncontrolled real estate growth results in the lack of basic infrastructures: buildings are constructed before water, electricity, or drainage systems are in place. Under the passivity of administrations and administrators, the liberalization of the land has promoted intensive and unchecked growth, and the preexisting tissue of the city is consequently being merged and forced against new residential plots. Today, diverse dwelling typologies and social classes co-exist in many areas with a stunning lack of amalgamation. This collision between the preexisting and the new, especially in the lack of services, leads to conflicts—mainly regarding waste management—that directly impact the river Someş that weaves through the city.

Repeatedly, inhabitants of the Florești neighborhood informal areas are hired to sort out the garbage of new dwellings. However, they don't have any facilities to manage waste properly; they simply accumulate tons of waste in their yards. Most of these sites border the river, so the debris generally slides down to the water's edge, where the water flows and pulls it down into the river, disappearing from the sight of the city's inhabitants. This flowing dump streams to the city center, where large volumes of objects arrive continuously.

After getting off the bus, we start to walk toward the riverbanks. We knew some students were building several on-site structures, but we didn't know where they were, so we walked along the river shore in search of them. We see the first of the new buildings, poor in quality, scattered around the land. Behind them, we find informal Roma settlements. When we finally reach the river, we can see the first installation on the other side. Several wooden structures are integrated into the landscape and spread around the shore. All of them are scaled to humans, framing the landscape and inviting any passerby to witness the poor quality of the water and the extraordinary landscape surrounding the river. This sharp contrast between the current state of the river and the natural beauty of the biotope only serves to underline the necessity of projects like Someș Delivery.

The educational project engages with multiple agents: students, visitors, and neighbors, who are all

directly concerned with the river's health. We first met the students at the final site of intervention, where they were building the final installation for the Someș Delivery Festival of the following weekend. "We have been building the structures for the last ten days, and the neighbors were saying, 'don't leave this structure here: it won't last long'; but so far, nothing has been stolen from here," says one of the students working on the site. The students are convinced that only through design and by providing alternative physical examples will people change and be more open: "This is the main role of an architect, to shift people's perspective. Before, you couldn't see the river, and now you can sit above it."

The last installation is a cantilevered platform that extends over the river with two seating areas and a roof. It faces the river and the mountain: "The main purpose of this place is to sit here and wonder about life," one of the students, Răzvan Stanciu, tells us. The installations let the community interact with the river—mainly through observation—and, consequently, with each other by gathering around these installations. Seemingly, the community is not cohesive and thus needs a good excuse to get together. These installations can be this excuse; the best way to engage with them is by enjoying them. Razvan said: "To catch [the community's] attention, you only need to make the installations very accessible and beautiful; everybody likes a nice place to stay."

After visiting the sites, we go back to the city where we meet the organizational team of Someș Delivery in their headquarters: Marius Moga, Ioana Trușcan, and Cristina Bodnărescu. The project started as a delivery market; they

tell us, one that would allow for pedestrian streets around the river, revealing the lack of a meaningful relationship between the urban tissue and the river. After lengthy discussions with local authorities, they decided on an event-based format that included sustainability, river preservation, and alternative urban development activities. The result was a success, with many people engaging with the project. In addition, the street event ensured that a wider public learned about the relevance of topics of concern, such as the right to public space or access to water. Currently, the project has developed in two directions. On the one hand, Someș Delivery has focused on consolidating the festival. On the other hand, they are working on long-term strategies for environmental preservation and better ways of living in the city. Such an event-based method creates a substantive framework that allows for experiments in which residents, together with institutions, can explore their necessities and possibilities.

This project attempts to engage students through a contest in which they address specific areas with analysis and materials. Subsequently, students select the projects that spark their interests, which they further develop while introducing their ideas. The selected projects are executed by all volunteers, who take responsibility for managing the project phases and completing construction. Peer-to-peer learning develops trust, encouraging the community to take agency over their physical surroundings.

Someș Delivery is a layered project that has evolved throughout the years and can consider multiple issues at the same time: enacting youth engagement by inviting them to participate in the design and construction

process; mapping the river by intervening in different spots along its course; waste management by uncovering the river's state to the local community and negotiating with the entities who manage the river, both the events and long-term approaches; and water access through its street events. Someș Delivery works closely with administrations to establish a common framework for long-term solutions and specific actions. Historically, this is a complicated process because administrations have been skeptical of any form of collaboration. However, through persistence and time, Someș Delivery has fostered an extensive network of local communities and academic institutions as collaborators and supporters.

For Somes Delivery, building trust with the administrations who are directly involved in the management of the river—Administrația Națională "Apele Române" ("Romanian Waters" National Administration), Ministerul Agriculturii și Dezvoltării Rurale (Ministry of Agriculture and Rural Development), and the national electric companies—has been a slow process. Initially, the administrations refused to collaborate with Someș Delivery since existing regulations did not allow them to do anything around the river: the laws regulating water access and use are outdated and fail to recognize leisure or other non-extractive activities in the legal framework. After many discussions in which Someș Delivery tried to find a legal way to pursue their project, they decided to include and invite members of the administration to the jury so that they were empowered as part of the decision-making; only then could they get the necessary approval from all three parties. The first edition was in 2015, and, since then, with each passing year, it has become easier to contact administrations to set up the legal framework. Currently, several NGOs across Romania, MiniMASS and MaiMultVerde among them, are working toward funding a Water Council that can analyze water health and take action on water management.

The river and public waters are full of memories and experiences; there is always an emotional bond between residents and their rivers. The projects of Someș Delivery allow for the engagement of residents and foster capacity building throughout their process. This method makes their projects accessible to a wide range of people so that they might join and address their connections to water differently. For example, one might sit on a nearby bench and look at the waste flowing in the river's current, reflecting on the actions that have created this condition. One might also be compelled to engage with the teams, building installations along the way. It is important to create an aware community in any part of the process that showcases the possibility of another kind of future for the Someș river. It is Someș Delivery who, through their multimodal work, urges residents, activists, and institutions to work together towards establishing a national debate and action on water management in Romania.

MAIMULTVERDE

Marta Popescu

• 44° 26'N – 26° 05'E

We met Marta Popescu in a café in the Lizeanu area, close to her office. Marta is part of the non-governmental organization MaiMultVerde, which translates to "More Green" in English. The organization has been working across Romania for the last thirteen years, carrying out afforestation projects, biodiversity protection, environmental education, alternative transport, food waste prevention, and combating plastic water pollution. One of their main projects is Cu Apele Curate (With Clean Waters), initiated in 2019 as a call for involvement in reducing and preventing plastic pollution in Danube's water and is addressed to the authorities and members of local communities.

Marta shared with us a study by the University of Vienna: 4.2 tons of plastic are transported daily, an average of 1533 tons per year by the Danube. As a result, water flows accumulate vast amounts of plastic, leading to the destruction of aquatic biodiversity, a dramatic decrease in the quality of the water we feed on, and the deterioration of the landscape. The project is aimed at historical pollution through actions to collect the plastic in the riverbed and to prevent future discharges through extensive and long-term efforts such as creating a national platform to generate protocols for water health. Romania is the last country the Danube crosses before it reaches the Black Sea, where the plastics and waste from Germany, Austria, Hungary, Serbia, and Romania gathers. Within Romania, 90% of the rivers are tributaries of the Danube.

River banks are hard to access across the country. It is hard to take care of the waters when residents do not see or relate to them. During the communist period, the state buried the public waters of Bucharest and redirected their flow.

Often rivers were enclosed or buried by concrete walls, highways, etc. The approach of MaiMultVerde is to work as an enabler, engaging with local communities living near the rivers and working with them to raise awareness on the ground. These communities are the first ones to be affected by pollution, and it is often their specific local needs and issues that are key to addressing these problems on a larger scale. Locally, socio-economic issues are already pressing and complex, making it challenging to prioritize ecological problems with residents.

Besides direct action, MaiMultVerde also works on prevention through educational programs. Historically and culturally, there is little sensitivity towards the health of the waters in Romania. It is common for residents to throw away trash in the water, watching how it 'gets washed and disappears,' even if it never really does: the plastic travels to the Black Sea, and along the way, it decomposes into small pieces, affecting the flora, fauna, and also people. Plastic water pollution is an international issue, with predictions stating that, at the present rate, oceans will contain more plastic than fish by 2050. Clean Water educational programs are vital to analyzing specific local problems and generating a community that is both aware and has the tools to act directly.

The lack of a national strategy strongly impacts water and waste management. A general problem with Romania's rivers' structure is that many spaces are legally categorized as "no man's land." Neither public nor private, no one is responsible for their care and stewardship. However, according to the law, the sanitation of watercourses and their adjacent banks is the task of local authorities, who are also responsible for maintaining the cleanliness of lakes, ponds, and dams. The reality is that local waste collection systems are often not implemented correctly, with landfills uncontrolled and difficult to locate. A strong collaboration between local authorities, the Administrația Națională ‚Apele Române' ('Romanian Waters' National Administration) is necessary to stop ecological disasters—and to prevent new ones. Here, MaiMultVerde also works as an advocate at the national and local levels, working with authorities, environmental NGOs, and local action groups.

The Clean Waters project started in 2019 with ten community organizers along the Danube. In just three years, Clean Waters has grown to twenty-five headquarters on riverbanks where residents want to reduce plastic pollution by identifying and implementing the most suitable solutions. This combination, developed by MaiMultVerde, between local engagement and national coordination is crucial to developing, deploying, and maintaining successful future plans to fight water pollution throughout Romania.

THE DANUBE DELTA BIOSPHERE

Răzvan Crimschi

● 44° 13'N – 30° 10'E

Răzvan Crimschi lives and works in Sfântu Gheorghe, where he was born. Though he studied at the Faculty of Ecology and Environmental Protection at the Ecological University of Bucharest and has multiple specializations (such as natural grazing), most of his knowledge about the Danube Delta comes from his life experience and observations. He returned to this place, where he developed various activities in the Delta as a researcher and a guide.

The population density of the Danube Delta is the lowest in the whole of temperate Europe. People from different cultural backgrounds live here, mainly Romanians, Ukrainians, and Russians. Although there is often a complicated relationship between these ethnic groups at a global level, there is no hostile relationship between them within the Delta; their co-existence is harmonious—they share the same problems, experiences, and resources. The relationship between Europe and the Delta, however, is primarily one of exploitation; clashes erupt when resources are threatened and need protection. "The isolation of the villages and their rough surroundings make it challenging for people's hearts and minds to open as they are not used to kindness," Răzvan tells us. Although it can be difficult for residents to appreciate this place's natural surroundings and potential, with most of their time in the Delta spent working in harsh conditions, they are intimately aware of their surroundings. They live in the midst of nature and are finding ways of living in it.

Răzvan first met us for a coffee in the center of Sfântu Gheorghe, in one of the very few bars in the village. From the beginning, we appreciated his vast knowledge of the Delta's ecosystem; he knows all about the species inhabiting the Delta and their interconnected relations. This Delta is a unique and sensitive biosphere that is changing rapidly, vulnerable to climate, population, and water quality variations. The extractive economy developed in the area during the last thirty years has decreased the richness of this landscape and its waterways, and many species have been dramatically affected. These changes have a visible impact on the morphology of this transboundary biosphere. After explaining his position as a resident and a researcher, Răzvan suggests jumping into the waters and witnessing the many relations established between beings in this place: "The sun is already going down, and it will be cold very soon," he warns us. On the left side of the canal, there is a massive flock of birds flying above us, moving from their feeding to their nesting area. Every day, they move kilometers around the Delta, inhabiting all of the landscape; the region is their extended living scenario.

Many areas of the Delta are strictly protected from tourist tours; nevertheless, people don't usually follow the rules, and it is common to see visitors all around. We start to enter the Turkish canal, which goes twelve kilometers to the south and is one of the few remaining natural channels (by now, most of them are human-made). The way the artificial channels shape the water is far different from the natural morphologies and the impact of artificial channels is one of the Delta's main problems. The southern side of the branch is a dynamic area, rich in species and seasonal variations of dry and wet land; this is why it is restricted, and this is how most of the natural channels are preserved.

The high crown trees are one of the examples of the interconnectedness of species in the Delta that Răzvan shares with us: "This is black alder; it is an essential and rare tree. It originally grew in the mountains; how it arrived here is a mystery. Still, here it survives with its roots completely submerged in the water, and it is only because of this lower vegetation that it manages to float," Razvan tells us. These trees depend entirely on the rest of the vegetation for nourishment and the dry land; that is why the disappearance of natural channels is significantly damaging for this species.

The tropical crawler *Periploca graeca*, commonly called Silkvine, is a vine that used to live exclusively in tropical climates. It is thought to have arrived in the Danube from the stomach of a migrating bird. As soon as the species arrived, it took hold in the Delta, developing novel strategies to overcome the winters. Although the specific mechanism is not clear yet, one of the explanations is that it became a parasitic plant by entering its seeds into the cork of existing trees. Răzvan shows us: "This is a water chestnut; it has a root system that goes to the bottom to fix the plant and has floating devices." He takes one plant and shows us the detail of this fixative device. It resembles a small, inflated sponge and gives them the capability to float. Because they can support a lot of weight, these connected plants are able to form and build platforms that birds use as nesting areas where their seeds can be eaten. "It is genuinely fantastic," Răzvan exclaims, "to see how every element supports other life structures!"

. The Danube River has three distributary branches, the Chilia, Sulina, and Sfântu Gheorghe, being the oldest. This is, in part, why most of the migratory fish—80% of the migration comes from the Black Sea—naturally use Sfântu Gheorghe as their path upstream. It is also the case that fishing developed in the Black Sea and these river waters; large quantities of fish are extracted from this region, representing a significant percentage of the economy. We arrive at what was once the old fishery of the Sfântu Gheorghe area and the biggest in Romania. Built in the 1950s, it is currently for sale. Behind the fishery, where they sorted, processed, and sold fish, there is the ice room that was covered externally with sand and internally with reeds to keep the temperature low. During winter, they would cut blocks of ice from the river to fill the reed-lined room; with the structure of the reed's stalks acting as such an efficient natural isolator, they managed to keep the ice until the following winter. The fishery is the legacy of large-scale fishing promoted during communism. But even with the transition to capitalism, it remains symbolic of a local economy based on the literal extraction of natural resources.

Throughout the tour, the conversation merged and ebbed with many accompanying birds while Răzvan would point to them, describing their qualities and sharing his knowledge of their behavioral patterns. The sun began to set, and we made our way back to the village. It was also sleeping time for the birds, except for the nocturnal ones, who hunt all night long. "To live here is equally unique and hard," Răzvan reflected. "You spend your days entirely wet for no money. Luckily, people do start to enjoy the beauty of this place." Back in the village—and dry—we reflected on our day and everything we came to know, and watched the sun set alongside the birds, the mosquitos, and Răzvan.

ASOCIAȚIA 37

Maria Luiza Zamora

● 45° 01'N – 29° 09'E

Maria Luiza Zamora is the founder of Asociația 37, a non-governmental organization based in Bucharest but operating in Dunavățu de Jos. Although Maria Luiza has a background in art history and national architectural heritage, she decided to focus on projects with an environmental focus in the Danube Delta. Her program, Delta Curată (Clean Delta), is linked to Cu Apele Curate (With Clean Waters) and a local school in Murighiol, where Asociația 37 is developing a regional educational program to raise awareness of water health, waste management, and recycling programs in the context of the Delta. Monthly, the association gathers with the local community, and they navigate the river's channels in search of litter. On the way, they talk to local fishermen or tourists about the urgency of keeping the basin and surroundings clean and healthy. This program also develops cultural activities where artists and students are engaged to mediate between issues of waste. Thus, the local community intervenes in the landscape through creative approaches while creating bonds among initiatives, local agents, and residents.

Maria Luiza receives us in her family home, a traditional wooden house; the garden has direct access to one of the branches of the Danube Delta. On our way, as we passed through villages, we noticed that almost all access to the river is privately owned, making it difficult to reach the water if you don't hold property. As a result, wastelands appear scattered throughout the landscape, with everything making its way to the waters in the channels: grey waters, trash, dead animals, and unwanted objects.

The central goal of Asociația 37 is to establish active local communities, especially the younger population, that have the autonomy to take care of their landscapes. Since local and regional administrations do not take responsibility for the primary water and waste management, it is critical to implement programs reinforcing population empowerment. In this regard, the main challenge Asociația encounters is that residents, due to their precarity and lack of infrastructure in the region, are hindered in their ability to focus on anything other than survival. This manifests in a general lack of interest in the environment they live in, compounded by the fact that their economies are based on fishing, boat tours, and, previously, hunting.

Water for this rural population may be their life, but it is also a neglected body. The Danube Delta may have been a UNESCO World Heritage Site since 1991, but local people are not always aware of it. Such a designation means little, if anything, to them. There is a significant gap between knowledge of their ecosystem and the biological value of the extraordinary nature surrounding them. This gap may seem surprising since many institutions are studying the Delta's biosphere (for example, the Murighiol Research Laboratory from the National Institute of Research and Development for Biological Sciences); however, as Maria

Luiza so succinctly asks: "they never engage with the local population, and they don't have educational programs; how will people appreciate and acknowledge the value of something they don't understand?"

For Asociația 37, this lack of understanding is the fundamental issue to be addressed. To them, it is necessary to educate and disseminate the issues facing the Danube Delta in an accessible language so that residents understand and acknowledge the natural treasure they are living within. Asociația 37's methodology is clear: they promote peer-to-peer relations and work with residents on topics such as understanding the Delta as a resource and learning cultural and biodiversity preservation. People learn how to recycle, how to reduce the use of plastic, and how to engage in critical consumption. For children, the focus is on early education, where they are given the knowledge and tools to comprehend the Delta as an ecosystem. Children are also encouraged to take care of the Delta actively; they enjoy going into the channels to clean it up by collecting litter, they talk with residents to raise awareness, and they learn to take care of the waters from their early years. There is hope to be found in educating future generations on the river's health and biodiversity issues. Currently, Asociația 37 is developing an artistic program whereby they hope to invite national artists to collaborate and reach an even broader audience by developing techniques of representation and dissemination of the value of the Danube.

IDENTITIES

BREAK

A CONVERSATION WITH MIHAI DANCIU

● 45° 25'N – 23° 22'E

Mihai is an architect and an urban planner, currently a professor at the Faculty of Architecture and Urbanism of the Universitatea Politehnica Timișoara (Polytechnic University of Timișoara). In addition to his academic activity, he is also engaged in several projects that research urban planning at the threshold of social science and design. In his approach as an architect, he is concerned with urban and community management, dedicated to an unconventional approach to urban planning. To date, his work is based upon his foundational belief that sustainable development must combine bottom-up and top-down approaches, such as those projects that start in the community and are later implemented by public administrations. Since 2013, he has taken part in the establishment of six associations as well as a coalition of non-governmental organizations (NGOs) from the Valea Jiului (Jiu Valley), encouraging the participation of all in decision-making processes. For him, community-based processes are needed as the first step for the furthering of any successful professional projects.

Mihai, for the last nine years, you have been working in the Banat region; what is your interest in spatial disciplines within the context of Timișoara and its surroundings?

MD Since I finished my studies in 2013, I began to develop a local critical urban practice by engaging with several initiatives aimed at increasing the quality of life by increasing the quality of the built environment. First, we realized that the architecture bureau of Timișoara needed a radical change to accomplish this goal. Then, as we studied the history of the Banat region, we found many interesting possibilities. The Banat is an intriguing region because of the convergence of several cultures; nowadays, it reaches Serbia, Hungary, and Romania. It has many common characteristics and unique regional developments: the three countries are connected through strong cultural ties. Recovering this area's cultural and architectural legacy can allow us to reframe our regional bonds through our shared past and, hopefully, a better future.

In the case of Timișoara's capital of the old Banat, urban development is recent; it was built 305 years ago under the vision of a great Austro-Hungarian city. Consistent with the practice of that time, any preexisting form was demolished and rebuilt from scratch. Foundations and traces of the previous culture were erased, and the only consideration was the then-present concerns of population, migration, agriculture, and manufacturing. The new plan consists of a center surrounded by a concentric design extending outwards and is entirely different from Turkish urban patterns representing the values and thinking of the then-new Empire. The process of erasing previous histories and cultures is noticeable: Timișoara appears to be a very young city. Thus, it is necessary to study this region and its policies to unfold its multicultural legacy and urban and rural developments.

Since 2013, I have been closely engaged with the Jiu Valley development. The topics have been varied, from recognizing the quality of rural architectural heritage in the Valley area, organizing events on the Petrila Coal

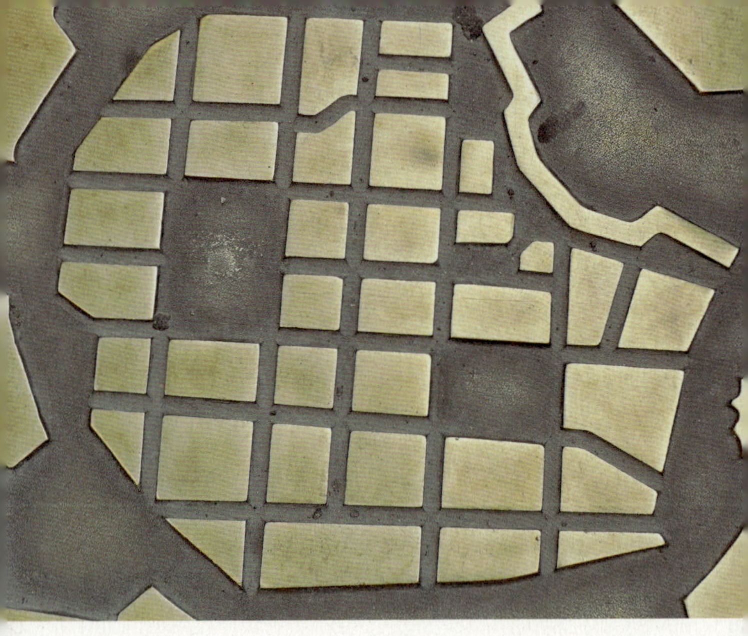

Mine ensemble site, or realizing projects for improving architectural and urban development. In addition, I also carried out educational activities, participatory urbanism, social research, and student projects in the Colonie neighborhood of Petroșani, where I have my practice to develop these projects.

What has been the focus of your research in the Banat region in recent years?

MD My grandmother is from this region and so I am particularly attached to it. This area has been a historical border between Romania and Hungary, highly militarized partially because of the coal exploitations and the mountains marking a natural border. I studied the Banat area for several years, specifically the case study Jiu Valley as part of The Coal Regions in Transition Platform developed by the European Commission. I am a working group member and actively participate in regular events. In this context, we carry out our civic activism activities in the Jiu Valley in multiple fields. I am also part of a project focused on the cultural landscapes in Banat, which aims to understand and highlight the particularities of cultural landscapes in western Romania by overlapping objective (geographical) and subjective (socio-cultural) characteristics. My research began as an investigation of the possible uses of this space beyond commodification and production. It developed by engaging the local community to envision viable frameworks, organizational models, and programs to build this underdeveloped region otherwise. As a result, I started working with a small community in this area, focusing on heritage and assisting them in using their own urban and natural resources to get out of the margins and find alternative economies to mining.

This project led me to truly come to know the Jiu Valley, where much of the population is poor and isolated. Moreover, there is a significant integration problem because many feel uprooted as numerous workers were forcefully brought there from other parts of the country during the communist regime. Further, they have variegated ethical backgrounds. Consequently, I have been developing several projects in this valley encouraging community engagement to improve living circumstances and reassess social ties. In the projects I am engaged with, the aim is to empower the community, to help them understand their resources and how to utilize them through cooperation, despite the scarcity of administrative help or possible frictions emerging from cultural differences.

Could you share with us some examples of the projects you have been engaged with and how they developed through time?

MD One great example is Planeta Petrila, a former coal mine of 16 hectares; it is the only one of this scale in the area. Starting in 2017, I became involved in the volunteer activities of the Planeta Petrila project, materialized by the establishment of the Planeta Petrila Association in 2019 and the monitoring of the urban regeneration project of the Mina Petrila ensemble. Previously, in 2015, they managed to stop the demolition of the infrastructure by reclaiming its heritage value and the right of former workers to use the facilities. It includes several remarkable buildings from the nineteen century; it is a magnificent

IULIAN și MARIA CÎRMAȚ

industrial complex! Once they paralyzed the demolition process, we started developing a very intricate bottom-up regeneration project.

These kinds of projects are not common in Romania; since 2012, we have been researching the area at many different levels taking the lead on how and what could be done with Planeta Petrila to promote alternative uses and economies, prioritizing the cultural development of the valley. The regeneration process has been developed mainly with private sponsorships because the state doesn't invest funds in heritage protection. We combine components of participatory urbanism, adaptive reuse, and regeneration through culture with strategies inherited from urban planning and strategic management. The main objective is to transform the former mining premises into a socio-economic center for a regenerated Jiu Valley. The community is regularly questioned about the possible uses of the former coal mining buildings. And so, depending on the topics raised, we develop a series of viable alternatives from a functional or constructive point of view. Then, out of the workshop-type processes, we invited the community to present its critical point of view.

So far, it has been a successful process with international recognition; for example, we are close to having a Europan competition site for the forthcoming editions. In 2017 I moved to Petroșani to start a program of public activities with the neighbors, teenagers, and children. We wanted to show that those spaces have been adapted for all kinds of cultural activities, including intersectional publics, to make visible the importance and potential for transitioning from old structures and their uses to new models of living together. In a region with contiguously built-up areas, it is difficult to establish such a direct relationship between mining complexes and the community's needs. However, in the town of Petrila, residents depended on Mina Petrila, which is why they are now looking for a new identity—including an economic one—developed around and through the heritage of the mining ensemble.

In Planeta Petrila, it is remarkable to see how many actors are involved in the process. How has the negotiation process been between residents, experts, the administration, and the private sector?

MD The evolution and negotiations of the project have been long and challenging mainly because of the property rights. It is a former mine, so the built area still belongs to the private sector, in this case, the mining company. However, the law does not allow the mining company to transfer it to the local administration without payment, and the administration does not have the money to acquire it. Therefore, we brought the issue to the council, a supra-administration, to see if they had the economic resources and the competence to buy it. We are currently in the process of finalizing the purchase, so, at the moment, the project and activities are on hold. In this context, we aim to generate a more agile bureaucratic structure to continue the regeneration process of the Jiu Valley, allowing us to integrate and coordinate the actors involved. As a result, we created the Coaliția Valea Jiului Implicată (Jiu Valley Engaged Coalition), in which twenty-one NGOs without political ties came together to form the largest coalition of mining communities in Europe.

Together, they are cooperating to build upon alternative models regarding social assistance, tourism, cultural projects, education, urban experimentation, and heritage. Moreover, from 2021 until 2030, the Asociația Pentru Dezvoltare Teritorială Integrată Valea Jiului (Association for Integrated Territorial Development Jiu Valley) will coordinate the process of a fair transition in the Jiu Valley.

For such a place, in search of a post-industrial meaning, I think we have developed the most agile structure possible, supported by local municipalities, the county public authority, the University of Petroșani, business representatives, and three local NGOs. For us, there is now the opportunity to create a solid project that tackles the main concerns in the region, enabling alternative and sustainable models. We are now applying for funding to continue the process we began, distributing these funds in ways that can further enhance the development of a consensual model for all involved. In this process, we also distinguished between different project areas and organized subgroups according to the needed experts from each field: ecology, urban development, local businesses, and social assistance. Within each project area, we must engage as many local agents as possible so the outcomes of these processes meet their actual necessities and can be sustained through time.

The project on cultural landscapes in Banat addresses many of the spatial practice issues, including organization models, community engagement, and the actualization of spatial typologies. How do you apply this tacit knowledge and practical experience within academia? And more specifically, could you elaborate on Triplex Confinium, the European research project?

MD Triplex Confinium is a supra-national project on the cultural and natural heritage of the former Banat region that is now divided between Hungary, Serbia, and Romania. Within the Triplex Confinium project, I worked closely with Bogdan Demetrescu (of the Universitatea Politehnică Timișoara) on developing a territorial exploration module within the 2021 Summer School. Now, together with Ștefana Bădescu (also of the Universitatea Politehnică Timișoara), we are working with Irina Tulbure (Universitatea de Arhitectură și Urbanism 'Ion Mincu' in Bucharest) to develop a teaching course on the historical evolution of the territory of Banat, and a methodology applicable in similar territorial circumstances. We are identifying common problems and gaps, building a platform to collaborate and take collective action on architecture and urban planning issues in this area, and studying future development possibilities.

The aim is to combine each partner country's spatial policies and educational trends by acknowledging that difference is just as important as sameness. In architecture schools, there is a tendency to tackle curricular gaps and mismatches between studies and current challenges in practice regarding local contexts. For example, partner universities work on the issue of transnational spaces and the impact of national borders on the development of local communities in bordering areas. In the process, there is a collaboration with grassroots initiatives working on the same topics trying to connect them with international networks so they can find economic and managerial support to develop their work.

> After going through projects based on community engagement, rural identities, or the actualization of spatial practice, we would like to know your thoughts on the issue of *property* in the context of Romania and how it affects the development of the *commons* as a threshold and an opportunity.

MD After the transition, several anomalous cases arose regarding property. This is a consequence of the liberalization of the territory that has led to the major privatization of previously publicly-owned land. This lack of regulation is indeed a burden to any urban strategy at a regional scale, and we usually face successive problems; we have no option but to work with this reality, acknowledge the specific conditions of this country, and rely on negotiations and establish platforms for mediation.

Concerning public spaces, I believe maintenance in Romania is similar to that of public spaces elsewhere. In my childhood, before the communist period, I remember that the community gathered neighbors from different nationalities and cultural backgrounds to work once per month on maintaining common areas. Moreover, during the communist period, several infrastructures and spaces were built by communities like schools and social centers, though mainly in rural areas. At that time, the state funded and maintained these common spaces and infrastructures. The state currently owns these public spaces but invests little capital for sustenance. Therefore, people have come to care less about them.

The reality is that nowadays, property boundaries are more rigid after the regime's fall. For example, we built a small community center as an annex to a public building in Petroșani; the plot occupies privately owned land. This project has been subject to intense negotiation about land property rights with the community. The council owns the main building, but the land is privately owned, and the owner does not want the building on his share of the land. Here comes the reality: the land is privately owned, so the council has no right to use or build on it. This is not a unique problem: it is common in many rural areas after the rapid transition and liberalization of land ownership.

Your practice expands ideas of what an architect or urban planner is. Beyond designing, you act as a mediator between different agents and play a critical role in education. How do you define your approach within the spatial discipline?

MD I appreciate this question. And thank you for the acknowledgment. As a member of several multidisciplinary teams, I work according to the typology and specifics of each project because needs are diverse and exist at distinct scales. But, for example, let's consider the last edition of the architecture biennale in Venice; *How will we live together?* In my opinion, it lacked any kind of construction or design of what is considered classical architecture. Where is the architecture? Most of the projects showcased in the biennale are somehow missing tangible details and results. This becomes problematic because they don't unfold over time and are somewhat ephemeral in their materiality. We have to work to translate strategies into practice. Multidisciplinary teams should focus on future urban developments and tackle the main social, natural, or economic issues while employing effective long-term design solutions.

AMBULANȚA PENTRU MONUMENTE

● 45° 22'N – 21° 42'E

We drive across the Banat region, meeting the qualities of this landscape, variegated villages, and cornfields along the way. We are on our way to one of the ongoing projects of Ambulanța Pentru Monumente (Ambulance for Monuments). This region is characterized by the historical legacy of three cultures: Austro-Hungarian, Ottoman, and local ethnicities representing the current geographical confines of Romania, Hungary, and Serbia. Besides these political limits, the boundaries of cultures and landscapes are diffuse, with this region gathering around sixteen minorities historically living together. At first sight, we can still see historical traces of each village's planning, often depending on which ancestor built it. For example, the Habsburgs imposed system of grid planning for villages of all ethnic groups and across the Banat region, which is recognizable thanks to family names engraved into the facades of the buildings or the grid urban tissue. Economically, it is an area based on industry and extensive agriculture. However, industrial exploitations have been mostly abandoned today, and residents are limited to making their living in modest economic terms through agricultural production.

After a restless trip beneath the rain, we arrived at Bocșa, ready to meet Mihai Moldovan and the Bocșa Montană blast furnace. Mihai is the project manager of Ambulance for Monuments Banat: they are roaming the Romanian countryside, calling on the aid of local people, together with architecture students, to repair endangered architectural heritage. First, they catalog the local heritage of the Banat region and identify the most damaged buildings. Then, they get in touch with local agents and institutions to work together, and they develop emergency conservation work to prevent the collapse of the structures and ensure the most relevant elements are safe. The Ambulance project aims to preserve the conditions of heritage buildings and raise awareness of their legacy by researching the rich cultural heritage of the Banat region.

The town is near Reșița, an area characterized by robust industrial development in the eighteenth and nineteenth centuries, and where the Reșița steel industry is closely linked to the construction of the Bocșa Montană steel plant, the building in which they are intervening: the steel plants in Reșița are considered twins of those in Bocșa. The Bocșa plants were built in 1869, but they had deteriorated since 1890 when the furnace was demolished and converted into a hydroelectric plant. In recent years, the monument lost its roof, and sections of the brick-bearing walls began to weaken, with cracks appearing and losing their load-bearing capacities. The Ambulance decided to start a rescue process in the summer of 2021, focusing on reconstructing the ceiling and weakened structural elements. For three weeks, volunteers from all over Romania, comprised mostly of architecture students, came to secure the building.

The main concept of Ambulance is not simply to save the monument; they are mostly trying to engage local communities and authorities in the project. Usually, the agreement is based on local authorities providing accommodation and meals with the NGO bringing know-how and materials. During the construction process, they generate a public program with workshops and conferences to establish as many entry points as possible

for the community. For example, in Bocșa, they hosted a film festival during the summer. Conviviality is the most important part of the project to enrich community-building and ensure the continuity of each intervention in a long-term projection.

The Ambulance has developed its methodologies through an educational framework, using traditional hands-on and peer-to-peer learning methods. Often, they work without electricity, refraining from using cement or other toxic materials. These conditions can turn the methods into craft-based work where the restoration students use traditional, generally more sustainable techniques, while also maintaining their cultural legacy. Unfortunately, these techniques are disappearing from generation to generation, so engaging young students have the potency of enabling its adaptation and continuity in the present. For example, in Bocșa Montană, they have worked on reconstructing the roof structure and ceiling, preparing the wooden beams one by one, and reassembling them up on the roof. In addition, they repaired the structurally damaged walls by replacing units and closing the cracks. In this way, they never turned down an entire part of the building but tried to overhaul each element, keeping the original materials.

After visiting the central nave, we walk downstairs to an annex with no roof, with the constant sound of water pouring from the rain and through the cracks of the bearing wall. On the other side of the wall is a dam; all the water flows through the cracks to the interior of the hydraulic machinery, flooding the area and remaining steel elements. This device turned several blowing machines

in the main nave through transmission belts. After the furnace was demolished, the system provided electricity to the town of Bocșa. During the tour with Mihai, students were scattered around the building, deeply engaged in their work; they barely gave us any attention and seemed autonomous and joyful. Later, we went to the main tower, where they built a scaffold to reach the highest part to repair the roof. Mihai told us: "We have a lot of fun every day climbing to the top with the students. They really like it."

Villages in this area are isolated, and people from outside rarely come to visit or interact with the communities. The young people generally migrate to the closest cities, like Timișoara, so many of the inhabitants of the small villages are adults and elderly. Consequently, building a relationship with the residents takes patience. The Ambulance for Monuments group tries to connect with people through day-to-day interactions, mingling at the main bar or local coffee shop, talking to the grocery manager, or sitting in the cafe and chatting with the customers. It takes time to build a relationship. It takes time to earn their confidence. Sometimes they go around the town, talking and explaining to the neighbors what they are working on. Gradually, when the community understands their goals and activities, they start contributing to the project from their perspectives and according to their capacities.

Romanian heritage and conservation efforts depend on the Ministry of Culture, although they are, in fact, based on volunteer work, non-governmental organizations, and private foundations. This dependency makes for precarious work and resources. In addition, the lack of administrative attention impacts people's interest in the sites, as seen in the neglect of the value of this region's heritage by both authorities and residents. However, as soon as the groups of volunteers start to act and work with the monuments, everyone comes to recognize the relevance of preservation and acknowledges the value of the work of the Ambulance. "It takes action to convince the local actors to get involved, but after the building is secured, they get to be in control of the afterlife of each building," says Mihai. The Ambulance teams assist with ideas and methods for community engagement; however, the continuity of the buildings is not their primary task. They keep in contact with the communities and facilitate support for the project through funding applications or constituting the associations that run the space. Still, their capacities are limited, so they must leave for the next emergency once the building is safe.

After the tour, we went to have lunch with Mihai and the students at the Council building and we see the good relationship they have with one another. The development of hands-on experiences with the students allows thinking and learning about architecture and construction in ways that emphasize the preservation and betterment of common goods. When spatial practice is connected to real problems, learning, and present life, transformative processes arise. The meaningful use of tools and capacities requires connecting the Ambulance practice to real problems—and people's lives.

H.ARTA

Anca Gyemant

● 45° 45’N – 21° 13’E

We meet with Anca in the Piața Unirii (Union Square) in Timişoara. It is a circular square with greenery in the middle that two gardeners are pruning; the conversation flows while they follow repetitive circles, mowing the grass. h.arta is a group of three women artists (Maria Crista, Anca Gyemant, and Rodica Tache) whose projects focus on producing knowledge and alternative educational models through a feminist approach. They employ different forms and formats, such as events, discussions, publications, and everyday actions, in order to create new spaces for political expression. Over the last ten years, h.arta has been active in two domains: the organization of exhibitions, meetings, debates, and workshops in the former h.arta space in Timişoara (founded as a not-for-profit), and a string of knowledge-sharing projects outside of the gallery, involving artists and students from Timişoara and beyond.

h.arta's methodology is based on friendship, which they understand as an everyday negotiation of differences, a way of learning from each other, and a political statement on the power of solidarity. The three—Maria, Anca, and Rodica—live together as a family beyond heteronormative family relations and without an official social contract; their friendship has the same value as any other relationship with a partner or other biological family members. They use art as a tool or a method by which to analyze contexts and address specific issues. And although they are not interested in being labeled as artists or activists, their work holds the characteristics of both. The connection between these characteristics is reflected in the pedagogical aspect of their work. The educational context allows them to generate a space for action where artistic practice becomes especially relevant. Younger people have not yet fully shaped their way of thinking but still have the flexibility to shape other patterns. This potency to change is a source of hope that directly impacts our societies. Preserving an inclusive, open school is at the core of h.arta's thinking and practice. Their artistic practice is a medium to generate critical thinking and to represent a plurality of voices integrating educational environments.

The legacy of previous generations and the interwoven stories and patterns is one of h.arta's fields of research. This research is especially relevant when talking about the end of worlds—those moments when one model collapses, and another rises. Anca explains how Romania has witnessed major transitional processes over the last fifty years: *Group Project*, an ever-evolving work, focuses on the shift from a communist past into the beginning of capitalism. By collaging analog photograph family portraits, they generate a real-fictional space, blending time and family ties and rebuilding family stories. *Group Portrait* tells the story of the lives of three generations of women—their grandmothers, mothers, and themselves—all connected to regime change and its impact at both personal and socio-political levels. With this project, h.arta visualizes the experiences of women who have lived in Romania in the previous century, rebuilding a collective story of personal and shared, common memories connected to specific socio-political transitions. "By now," Anca reflected, "everything is written under a demonizing perspective of what communism was. Yes, it had its terrible sides, but anything that was emancipatory for society has been erased." h.arta considers their generation's memories of what it was like to be a child under that communist regime. "[I] don't want to romanticize that time, but I remember seeing a picture of a homeless person in a foreign magazine, and I was shocked; I didn't know such a thing existed; everyone had shelter."

Such memories are valuable as they reveal other, forgotten aspects of communism: in their work, it is essential to know both what was gained and what was lost. Nowadays, mainstream discourse and conversations often lack a clear understanding of how the transition from socialism to capitalism transpired and how it affected public services and spaces. Anca believes the rapid liberalization of the public sector has been problematic in many ways; for example, the gap between the claims of freedom right after the fall of the regime and the aftermath of the accession to capitalism developed into a lack of access to basic needs like housing, labor, and schools.

Through their practice h.arta tries to connect the past and the present, reaffirming the relevance and necessity of building feminist narratives and visions through artistic and educational practices.

AICI ACOLO POP-UP GALLERY

Edith Lázár and Flaviu Rogojan

● 46° 46'N – 23° 35'E

We spoke with Edith Lázár and Flaviu Rogojan from Aici Acolo Pop-Up Gallery, a project to support young and emerging artists by organizing pop-up exhibitions that transform unused or abandoned urban spaces into temporary art spaces. The project arose in 2014 from the necessity of finding alternative art galleries or workshops in the city of Cluj-Napoca. At the time, the young art scene in the city was growing, but it was difficult to access the local artistic context. The Aici Acolo team decided to create something in this missing context that could integrate local young artists into the art scene, offering them the opportunity to present their work to a broader audience while exploring their interests and research topics.

"Our initial aim was to exhibit the works of as many young artists as possible, to offer them visibility," Flaviu told us. Considering the lack of infrastructure and economic resources, they focused their efforts on addressing the needs of the young artist generation. As a result, they decided to create a pop-up format that they believed could make the project sustainable over time. Aici Acolo began renting spaces for upcoming events and exhibitions. The places were accessible from the street, so any passer-by could see and enter, regardless if they were part of the art world. This pop-up format allowed for working in diverse settings and creating unique shows, making this project even more extraordinary.

When they began, the Aici Acolo team thought it would be effortless to rent spaces: "In Cluj, a few years ago, there were many empty spaces in the middle of the city. We thought everyone would be willing to rent their empty places for this purpose," Édith told us. At the time, the Aici Acolo team thought these short-term uses could activate the place and generate a cultural value while enabling a dynamic urban fabric accessible to young artists. "We saw it as a perfect match, but unfortunately, that wasn't the case; everyone wanted money," says Flaviu. Now the city has developed, undergoing a fast process of gentrification, and they recognize the naivety of their thinking. The context of the current crisis and the rise of real estate prices has made it progressively harder to find affordable locations. As a result, it seems that the primary objective of their work failed to materialize: they could not complete or sustain the project.

The outcome of this process is now a map of empty spaces, many still on hold. This map shows how the city lacks accessibility and excludes a diversity of actors. For this reason, and intending to continue the project in another form, Aici Acolo is shifting its efforts. Where they first tried to showcase as many artists as possible, they now focus on fewer artists, putting more energy into the content of the shows and the infrastructure their artists need. In this new project phase, they concentrate on taking care of the artist's needs and the narratives they want to bring to the table. They further refined their concept by reducing the number of exhibitions, focusing on hosting artists who explore similar interests. They came to realize that artists are not merely lacking exhibition spaces but also spaces to work while being supported: the previous pop-up format wasn't responding to those needs. Today Aici Acolo's initiative is more refined and nuanced; hosting intensive residencies, experimental laboratories, and shows, they focus on the resources for production, closely following—and thereby supporting—each artist's process.

CASA VERDE

Silviu Medeșan and Tobias Pasăre

● 46° 55'N – 23° 09'E

In search of a more sustainable way of living and hoping to explore rural areas, Tobias and Silviu started Casa Verde, a project with Lóránt and Kinga Váradi. In essence, they bought a house and an old barn. Over a conversation that spans a day, they share their plans for the future of this project, their vision, and the challenges they see ahead.

We meet with Silviu and Tobias in the village of Petrinzel, one of the nine villages that comprise the Almașu commune in the Sălaj County of Romania. Part of Transylvania, the Sălaj is an ethnographical region with a range of cultures, though a predominantly Hungarian ethnicity. In the southern part of Sălaj is Țara Călatei (Kalotaszeg in Hungarian), a rural region influenced by remarkable craftsmanship. In the village, the principal public spaces—a church, a school, and a cultural community center—are currently abandoned. The demographics of this region are predominantly adults and older adults. Tobias and Silviu see great potential in collaborating with the local population to recover communal spaces while bringing new uses and interests in an intersectional development of the village. The decision to move out of the city was a direct consequence of the pandemic; Tobias and Silviu found that their needs and concerns as young individuals were no longer tied to an urban context. Instead, they see this rural environment as an opportunity to build bridges between perceived dichotomies of the urban and rural, young and old generations, and art and local crafts.

Tobias and Silviu, together with Lóránt and Kinga Váradi as Casa Verde are refurbishing the complex now: the house will hold a common living space, the barn will have an educational space, and a garden for vegetables.

Today, rural areas of Romania are undergoing a slow process of development compared to urban spaces. Tobias and Silviu plan to integrate Casa Verde as a place for meaningful exchanges between rural and urban knowledge and ways of living. As they work, they carefully learn the local context, opening up a dialogue with its rural identities, bringing together their urban resources and backgrounds with the legacies and crafts from the village through collective activities and, they hope, Casa Verde's future educational program.

The house is in the midst of being renovated. Earthquakes have damaged the structure, leaving extensive cracks. For Tobias and Silviu, the rebuilding process is a central part of the project, and they wish to use as few resources as possible to amend the structure using local techniques. The foundations and ground floor walls are made of stone, and the upper structure consists of wood and bricks; the covering of surfaces is adobe, all local natural materials, following Casa Verde's objective to recover the house with local crafts.

A driving idea behind Casa Verde is to retrieve local knowledge and legacies and combine them with contemporary topics and ways of doing; they want to investigate old crafts and embed them firmly in the present. There is already a legacy and repository of local crafts in the house, from ceramics to textiles and embroidery. These various elements represent local identities that Casa Verde aims to reinforce. In recent years, Tobias has been working on traditional embroidery that in its motifs address contemporary topics like queer activism and sustainability. He sees the potential of learning local folklore techniques while simultaneously implementing and inserting ongoing debates into the rural context. In this way, Casa Verde can be a space for shared learning between generations, valuing the vestiges inherited from the past with ways of knowing from the present for the future.

What characterizes the rural in this area is a lack of local economy. Residents struggle to find sources of work and money because almost every economic activity is centralized in the city. In addition, there is a generational gap. Tobias and Silviu don't want to romanticize the idea of returning to the countryside. Instead, they aim to contribute to improving conditions by carrying their tools from the city. Enabling common and shared spaces for knowledge and social exchange is crucial to doing this. Through Casa Verde, they envision a space for direct action, promoting ways of living that address issues that include homophobia, poverty, and climate change. By acting in this context, they unveil and confront issues not often broached by local communities. Working together with each other and with residents, they aim to highlight and examine global concerns in a local manner.

RADICAL

RITUALS

RITUALS

While expanding on the potency and patterns of rituals, we find ourselves embedded in the process of rehearsing this research *as* a ritual. The methodology of this project is intimately related to the act of traveling and being together, teams and actors engaged, allowing us to develop our own strategies and methods. Traveling along the line is our principal ritual, repeating in a sequence of documentation and post-production. In Radical Rituals 45°N 20°E – 45°N 31°E, this book chapter is dedicated to the rituals we developed and rehearsed. We will produce an index of practices shaped through time by gathering actions in each iteration.

We see rituals as a method of bringing together a community of actors. Each practice we feature, scattered in the landscape we travel through, has its own rituals. By gathering diverse local rituals, we want to showcase their shared characteristics with regard to the idea of transformation and agency; they all build patterns and rehearse other ways of acting until they consolidate among people directly engaged with each of the projects–ultimately shaping the space to where they belong. Now, the question is, how do we translate the foundations of those practices to a broader network of agents so that they can be adapted to other contexts? We yet don't have a straightforward answer to this question. Our strategy is to repeat sequences of research-rituals that will reveal the qualities of the distributed knowledge on time.

In our first iteration, we unfolded the following rituals by collecting stories, pictures, physical objects, and plants as traces of the landscapes we crossed.

Travelling and mapping, we always leave the path of our trip slightly open, so we can maneuver when unexpected encounters and locations appear, influencing our routes and outcomes. Through multimodal documentation, we take pictures and portraits of the protagonists and their locations of work. We also record the discussions and soundscapes.

Conversing and listening was essential to us as we rehearsed a practice of careful tending.

ritual
RADICAL

Instead of going to places with pre-conceived ideas, we listened to the protagonists. This way of approaching the work allowed the conversation to guide the content, and our questions arose from their topics and concerns. The conversation as a method and listening as an approach has been essential to reaching actors not necessarily belonging to the spatial discipline. Language can be exclusive, but deep listening rarely is.

For this research, the physical sphere is crucial. But how do we depict the physical qualities of each case study and the landscapes we encounter? We asked all of the actors we interviewed for physical objects, collected plants and soil, sand, and shells from the landscapes we crossed. The aesthetical qualities of each territory may be portrayed through other rituals in further iterations. Radical Rituals rituals are a catalog of methods and rehearsals that will grow and change along the way—an evolving and complementary index of empirical and exploratory research.

ACKNOWLEDGMENTS

forty five degrees would like to express our utmost appreciation to all of the protagonists featured in this volume. Not just for taking the time to guide us through their fantastic work but also for sharing so openly all their broad knowledge, welcoming us into their worlds, their wonders, and concerns. Traveling amid the pandemic has been challenging at times, but it wouldn't have been possible without the generosity of all the hosts that accompanied us along the way, and the institutions and actors that made us feel at home.

We would like to thank the publisher Radu Lesevschi, for his support and excitement in developing this project together. For the same reason, we thank our editor Elise Misao Hunchuck for accepting our invitation to join us in this venture and for her care-full and sharp eye. Katharina Hetzeneder, as a designer, gave shape to the materials sharply and superbly and has been a sensitive companion through the final process.

We would like to take the opportunity to thank Alex Axinte for his text contribution, helping us situate the addressed topics in the context of Romania. Oana Simonescu, for opening the doors of Faber along with a community of actors around Timişoara. Quim Pujol for his critical feedback in shaping the embryonic structure of Radical Rituals and Luna Bongers for her careful transcription and reviewing of the raw materials, helping us shape the final outcome.

This project has been generously supported by Akademie Schloss Solitude, Goethe Institute Bucharest, and ARC Bucharest. With their trust in this publication and research, and through their offering of a three-month residency in Romania, enabled by Akademie Schloss Solitude alongside the local partners in Romania through the Eastern European Network program, we were able to realize the first field trip—and now, this first publication. This phase would not have been possible without their open-handed contribution.

In short, this broad project has been possible thanks to the many actors engaged in conversations, hours on trains, boat rides, and critical thinking together. We hope to continue this exploration for many more years, together, with all of you.

IMAGE CREDITS

Pages 1, 14 (top and bottom), 18, 23, 26, 30, 34, 38, 39, and 42. Photographs by Berta Gutiérrez Casaos (2021). Film. Courtesy *forty five degrees.*

Page 46 (top). Photograph by Alex Axinte (2021). Digital. Courtesy Alex Axinte.

Page 46 (bottom). Still from an untitled film by Dan Dinescu (1984). Film. Courtesy Alex Axinte.

Page 52. Drawing by Alex Axinte (2021). Digital. Courtesy Alex Axinte.

Pages 56 and 57. Photographs of Drumul Taberei by Mihai Oroveanu (1973). From the Collection of Images Mihai Oroveanu, courtesy of Anca Oroveanu and Salonul de Proiecte. More can be found at www.photopastfuture.ro

Pages 61, 64, 70, 77, 81, and 84. Drawings by Alex Axinte (2021). Digital. Courtesy Alex Axinte.

Pages 88–89. Photograph by Berta Gutiérrez Casaos (2021). Film. Courtesy *forty five degrees.*

Page 90. Photographs (front and back) by Bianza Azap (2020). Digital. Courtesy BETA 2020.

Page 95. Photograph by Dan Purice (2020). Digital. Courtesy BETA 2020.

Page 98. Photograph by Alex Todirică (2018). Digital. BETA 2018.

Page 101. Photograph by Alex Todirică (2018). Digital. BETA 2018.

Page 103. Photograph by Alex Todirică (2018). Digital. BETA 2018.

Page 104 (top and bottom). Photographs by Berta Gutiérrez Casaos (2021). Film. Courtesy *forty five degrees.*

Pages 108, 111, and 112. Photographs by Alkistis Thomidou (2021). Digital. Courtesy *forty five degrees.*

Page 115. Photograph by Berta Gutiérrez Casaos (2021). Film. Courtesy *forty five degrees.*

Page 116. Photograph by Alkistis Thomidou (2021). Digital. Courtesy *forty five degrees.*

Page 117. Drawings by Silvia Moldovan (2019). Scan. Courtesy of Silvia Moldovan.

Page 119. Photograph by Berta Gutiérrez Casaos (2021). Film. Courtesy *forty five degrees.*

Page 121 (top and bottom). Photographs by Asociația MaiMultVerde (2020). Digital. Courtesy of Atelier Ad Hoc Arhitectura.

Page 122. Photograph by Frank Kleinbach (2021). Digital. Courtesy of Atelier Ad Hoc Arhitectura.

Page 124. Photograph by Berta Gutiérrez Casaos (2021). Film. Courtesy *forty five degrees.*

Pages 126 and 127. Photographs by Alkistis Thomidou (2021). Digital. Courtesy *forty five degrees.*

Pages 128–129. Photograph by Berta Gutiérrez Casaos (2021). Film. Courtesy *forty five degrees.*

Page 130 (front). Photograph by Berta Gutiérrez Casaos (2021). Film. Courtesy *forty five degrees.*

Pages 130 (back), 134 (top and bottom), and 138. Photographs by Cladiu Popescu (2019). Digital. Courtesy of Letea în UNESCO.

Pages 142, 146, 148, 149 and 151. Photographs by Alkistis Thomidou (2021). Digital. Courtesy *forty five degrees.*

Page 154. Photograph by MaiMultVerde (2019). Digital. Courtesy of Asociația MaiMultVerde.

Page 156. Photograph by Vlad Bâscă (2020). Digital. Courtesy of Asociația MaiMultVerde.

Page 158. Photograph by Berta Gutiérrez Casaos (2021). Film. Courtesy *forty five degrees*.

Pages 160 and 161. Photographs by Alkistis Thomidou (2021). Digital. Courtesy *forty five degrees*.

Pages 163 (top and bottom) and 165. Photographs by Berta Gutiérrez Casaos (2021). Film. Courtesy *forty five degrees*.

Pages 167 and 168. Photographs by Luiza Zamora (2021). Digital. Courtesy of Asociația 37.

Pages 170–171 and 172 (front and back). Photographs by Berta Gutiérrez Casaos (2021). Film. Courtesy *forty five degrees*.

Page 176. Photograph by Alkistis Thomidou (2021). Digital. Courtesy *forty five degrees*.

Pages 179 and 182. Photographs by Berta Gutiérrez Casaos (2021). Film. Courtesy *forty five degrees*.

Page 188. Photograph by Alkistis Thomidou (2021). Digital. Courtesy *forty five degrees*.

Page 192. Still from unknown film. Courtesy of Ambulanța pentru Monumente Banat.

Pages 193, 195, 196, and 199. Photographs by Berta Gutiérrez Casaos (2021). Film. Courtesy *forty five degrees*.

Page 201. Collage by h.arta (2008). Courtesy of h.arta.

Page 203. Photograph by Berta Gutiérrez Casaos (2021). Film. Courtesy *forty five degrees*.

Pages 204 and 205. Photographs by Alkistis Thomidou (2021). Digital. Courtesy *forty five degrees*.

Page 207. Photograph by Berta Gutiérrez Casaos (2021). Film. Courtesy *forty five degrees*.

Pages 209 and 210. Photographs by Alkistis Thomidou (2021). Digital. Courtesy *forty five degrees*.

Page 216. Photograph (detail) by Silke Briel (2022). Digital. *forty five degrees*.

Page 224. Photograph by Alkistis Thomidou (2021). Digital. Courtesy *forty five degrees*.

DISTRIBUTION

FRANCE, BELGIUM, LUXEMBOURG
Les presses du réel
35 rue Colson
21000 Dijon
France
www.lespressesdureel.com

GERMANY
Motto Distribution
Skalitzer Str. 68
10997 Berlin
Germany
www.mottodistribution.com

UNITED KINGDOM
Antenne Books
The Sunroom
17 Amhurst Terrace
E82BT London
United Kingdom
www.antennebooks.com

REST OF THE WORLD
Idea Books
Nieuwe Hemweg 6R
1013 BG Amsterdam
Netherlands
www.ideabooks.nl

PUNCH
Piata Pache Protopopescu 13 ap.4
021401 Bucharest
Romania
www.p-u-n-c-h.ro

COLOPHON

RADICAL RITUALS 45°N 20°E – 45°N 31°E
An itinerant survey along the 45°N parallel

A publication by *forty five degrees* (Berta Gutiérrez and Alkistis Thomidou)
Edited by Elise Misao Hunchuck

Publisher: PUNCH Press, Bucharest
www.p-u-n-c-h.ro
Instagram: @punch.bucharest

Copyeditor and proofreader: Elise Misao Hunchuck
Graphic designer: Katharina Hetzeneder

This book is printed on Circle Volume White 90g and Peyer Peytan 240g.
Printed by Gutenberg Beuys Feindruckerei GmbH in Langenhagen, Germany (EU).

© 2022 for texts and images, their authors

This book is licensed under a Creative Commons Attribution-NonCommercial-NoDerivatives 4.0 License (CC BY-NC-ND 4.0) of this edition by the publisher and the authors. It allows for sharing, but not commercial nor derivative use, of the material in any medium or format.

This publication is a result of *forty five degrees'* residency in Romania in 2021 organized by Arc Bucharest (www.arcbucharest.ro) in the frame of Akademie Schloss Solitude's Eastern European Network exchange program. The publication was realized with the support of Akademie Schloss Solitude, Goethe Institute Bucharest, and Administration of the National Cultural Fund (AFCN) of Romania.

PROIECT CO-FINANȚAT DE:

Every effort has been made to contact copyright holders and to obtain their permission for the use of copyright material. In the event any copyright holder has been inadvertently omitted, please contact PUNCH. Any corrections will be incorporated in future reprints or editions of this book.

ISBN: 978-606-95055-6-4